Tranquility
FOUNTAINS

Tranquility
FOUNTAINS

PROJECTS
FOR A
SERENE LIFESTYLE

Mickey Baskett

Sterling Publishing Co., Inc.
New York

Prolific Impressions Production Staff:

Editor: Mickey Baskett
Copy: Sylvia Carroll
Graphics: Dianne Miller, Karen Turpin
Styling: Lenos Key
Photography: Jerry Mucklow
Administration: Jim Baskett

Library of Congress Cataloging-in-Publication Data Available

Published by Sterling Publishing Company, Inc.
387 Park Avenue South, New York, N.Y. 10016
Produced by Prolific Impressions, Inc.
160 South Candler St., Decatur, GA 30030
©2001 Prolific Impressions, INC.
Distributed in Canada by Sterling Publishing
c/o Canadian Manda Group, One Atlantic Avenue, Suite 105
Toronto, Ontario, Canada M6K 3E7
Distributed in Great Britain and Europe by Cassell PLC
Wellington House, 125 Strand, London WC2R 0BB, England
Distributed in Australia by Capricorn Link (Australia) Pty. Ltd.
P.O. Box 6651, Baulkham Hills, Business Centre, NSW 2153
Australia

Printed in the USA
Sterling ISBN 0-8069-2759-3

CONTENTS

Learn to Construct Small Fountains From a Variety of Materials

Continued on next page

CONTENTS

29 Small Tabletop Fountains to Make For Your Personal Pleasure

*T*ranquility ... the very word comes out like water tumbling down a bed of well worn stones. If we could find a way to create tranquil movement in our noisy hectic lives, what would that moment be worth? This book will help you find that peaceful place where you can sit and listen. It's a small respite in a busy life...something to help you through your day, your week, your moment of stress. Imagine yourself sitting by a babbling brook on a sunny afternoon. Hear the water fall over the rocks and rush on down the mountain to the green valley below. Now, imagine that sound in your own home or office. Through this book you can create that wonderful peaceful moment of sitting by a small stream or brook...a small place on your table or bedside that reminds you of the quiet part of life. Create a small altar to the natural and wholesome things that make the world a beautiful place to be. You can fashion a space in your own environment that will take you away or bring you back to the serene state of mind that helps you concentrate and think clearly.

*W*ater symbolizes life itself. In fact, it doesn't just symbolize it, it creates it. Water is considered the building block of life. As scientists will tell you, where there's water, there's life. But it nourishes our souls as well as our bodies. It's an essential element of nature that sustains and renews us. Water heals and purifies. It cleanses and revives. Is it any wonder that it is a part of so many religious rituals, both ancient and current? In early Christian times, fountains were placed in the atrium court of the Christian basilica as symbols of purification. The ritual of purification also exists in the Shinto temples in Asian cultures. Many modern churches practice christen-ing or dunking in water (baptism) as one of the most important rites of their religion.

Water is the great solvent, dissolving barriers. We find this expressed in our philosophies, as well. To the *Feng shui* masters, it is the element of insight, motivation, and social contacts. As an astrological element, water represents feelings and emotions, as through these we cease to be separated from others but become part of the sea of humanity in which our barriers between each other are dissolved.

Water, therefore naturally became a great part of our art, expressed particularly in pools and fountains. Water has been at the center of society in most all cultures, from public baths, central drinking fountains, and private courtyard pools. In addition, the beauty of water is the subject of many a painting, poem, song or symphony.

*H*istorically fountains first appeared in Iran and the Middle East about 3000 B.C. They were of great importance to the community, especially the public drinking fountains. These fountains were simple in structure and were commonly just a spout and stone carved basin enclosed within a graceful niche. Fountains have certainly expanded and grown both in popularity and size since that time. The famous Fountains at the Palace of Versailles France are some of the most spectacular in the world. On a summer Sunday you can witness the magnificent scene of all the 18th century royal fountains erupting at once. The sunlit frothy water is forced high into the air and rains down into a clear pool below. The sight is something to behold. It is a great testament to the size and splendor to which fountain design eventually rose. Much simpler fountains more akin to the first ones of history still exist all over the world in picturesque villages and towns which have maintained their heritage.

*M*odern water art in fountains in the last decade or two has become highly sophisticated by adding the use of computers and utilizing the latest understanding of water's molecular nature. An arc of water can be made to look like a solid bar by aligning the molecules in a certain way. With computerized timing, such a "bar" can appear to jump from one spot to another. Computerized timing can also make jets of water keep time with classical music, as if the music were causing the water to dance. So today's water art is much more than the design of the fountain that contains the water. The water itself has become an art medium.

Pictured at right: An ancient public fountain in a French village.

𝓕*lowing* water is one of the most satisfying sounds we know. Our fascination for and magnetic affinity with this element is what inspires the creation of our own fountains for our homes. When you close your eyes and let the sound of the water from your fountain trickle through your subconscious, you float away from the present and meander down a stream of relaxation. Once you create the sound of water through a personal fountain, you will want to share that joy with others and spread that peace to many areas of your life. ❏

Pictured at left: A public fountain in Provence France.

MATERIALS
to Build Your Fountain

*F*ountains can be made for your home or office with just a few easy steps. Remember the following fundamentals and you will always be successful.

A pump is a necessary ingredient for a fountain. You will want to hide it but also protect it from too much weight or becoming clogged. Covering the apparatus that makes it a fountain can be just as fun as hiding Easter eggs. You are the only one who will know how you created the magic of your fountain.

Most fountain pumps today are electrical, so you will always need an **electrical connection**. The cord must come out of the fountain and must be plugged in. Once you get used to the fact that you MUST have a cord, you can get on with the creative and inventive ways to hide it. The main design feature in your fountain can cover or hide the cord, or you can use filler materials to achieve this.

Read the next few pages carefully and you will be able to create most any fountain you can imagine. The basics are not difficult, but there are some rules that should not be broken. As with any successful project, good preparation and knowledge will insure the outcome.

PUMPS

*P*umps are required. Every fountain moves water and needs a pump to do just that. However, pumps are small, harmless things that require almost no mechanical skill. If you can plug in a lamp, you can plug in a pump. Pumps are also relatively inexpensive (no more than dining out with a friend or partner at a fairly nice restaurant).

The kind of pumps used in this book are submersible pumps. They take the water in and shoot the water back out. The water you put in your fountain will be circulated through the pump as long as the pump is plugged in. Pumps will be designated for indoor use, outdoor use, or indoor/outdoor use. Be sure to choose the correct pump for your environment in this regard. Pumps can be found in most garden supply, home building supply or pool stores.

There are several parts to a pump and a few specifications you should know about. Once we explain these, you will know all you need to know about the pump part of your project.

Moving The Water: How Much & How High?

• **Water Height:** You must consider how high the pump will be able to shoot water into the air. For small indoor fountains you will only need one or two feet of maximum shooting capacity. On the pump you will see: H max 2ft. This tells you that the pump can shoot water into the air as high as 2 feet. You probably don't want to spew water twenty feet into the air unless you are creating your own indoor Versailles, and there's no reason to spend money on a height that's not needed. However, obstructions to the water flow will decrease the height. For example, if the water is going through some small openings and will encounter some friction, this will decrease the height of the water flow.

• **Gallons:** Another statistic on the pump is the GPH. This stands for Gallons Per Hour. Most pumps for these small projects will use approximately 80 gallons of water per hour. (For comparison, large fire hoses and irrigation system pumps use about 60 gallons per minute.)

• **Voltage:** The pump will also be labeled with a voltage statistic. All of the pumps for these projects should have a 3-prong plug and plug into a normal 120 volt household electrical outlet. Also available are dual-power pumps. These can be operated with a battery pack that requires "D" size batteries; or operate with electricity.

Parts of a Pump

• **Inflow:** You will see an intake filter on the pump where the water enters the pump. These must always be kept open and free of dirt and debris.

• **Outflow:** Also notice the out flow opening on the pump – the Outflow Post.. This is where the plastic tube is attached which will take your water to the correct position for flowing out of a spout or over the side of your rocks. Some pumps have the outflow post on top and others have it on the side. Consider this in relationship to your design. Which would work best?

• **Pressure Setting:** On most pumps there is a pressure setting, usually on the side. This controls the pressure of the water flow and allows for a faster flow or a slower trickle of water. You will want to test your pressure setting while your fountain is still unassembled. It is hard to take a fountain apart after it is all glued together and neatly arranged, just because you discovered that it throws water all over your good sofa. FILL the fountain container with water (temporarily), test the pressure setting, and set it at your chosen rate of flow before all the rocks and pebbles and plants are irrevocably placed. If the higher settings cause water to splash outside of your fountain onto furniture, lower the setting until the water is nicely contained in the fountain.

• **Off/On Switch:** Some pumps have the switch on the pumps. Others have a switch on the cord. If the pump will be difficult to access on your fountain design, consider a pump with the switch on the cord.

• **Cord:** The cord is the same kind of electrical cord with a plug on it that you are used to seeing on all your electrical appliances, except that it is waterproof. When purchasing your pump, you must consider the length of cord you need for where you want to display your fountain. Unlike many other appliances, you cannot replace the cord on the pump with another, longer one. The cords on these pumps have a waterproof seal and to replace it would destroy this seal.

• **Drip Loop:** ELECTRICITY AND WATER DO NOT MIX. Along these lines, it is important to have a drip loop on the cord so that any water that might drip from the fountain doesn't run straight down the cord into the electrical outlet. The drip loop is shown in Fig. 1 and Fig. 2.

Pump Tips

• There are features that can make your pump expensive but which are not necessary. Shooting capacity is the main one of these – the higher it shoots, the greater the cost. More shooting capacity than needed can, in fact, be a disadvantage in indoor pumps where you want to keep the water well contained in the fountain.

• If you are considering a pump that has a top outflow post and your design would work best with it on the side, it is sometimes possible to orient the pump so that the outflow post is on the side. You must just be sure that the water level will cover the pump sufficiently when it is turned that way. Also, most pumps have suction cups on the bottom which are very helpful because the pumps are light in weight. To reorient the pump would cause you to forego use of this feature.

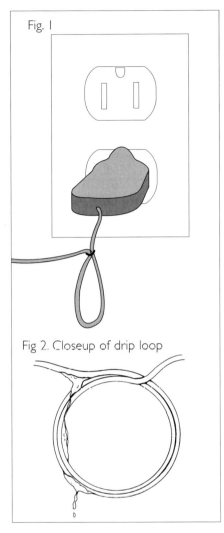

Fig. I

Fig 2. Closeup of drip loop

• **Never operate the pump without water** as the rotor is lubricated by water. The pump will operate best when completely submerged under water. The instructions indicate at least 3/4" water surrounding the pump, including above it.

• Keep a healthy respect for the electrical part of your project and do not allow water anywhere near the plug. On these pumps, the wiring is sealed off from moving parts and water and electricity are kept apart by a solid plastic wall as well as other seals.

• Noise: Some pumps are quieter than others. Most of the small magnet-driven fountain pumps are relatively quiet. Inexpensive aquarium pumps may be much noisier. If your fountain pump seems too noisy, make sure that it is centered in the pump housing and not touching the sides of the housing or touching rocks that create vibration. Make sure the rubber feet are in place and that the water level is full; otherwise, your pump may growl.

TUBING

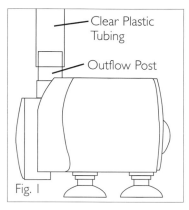

Clear Plastic Tubing

Outflow Post

Fig. 1

Tubing is made of plastic and is attached to the pump to carry your water out of the pump and up and over your chosen design features. Fig. 1 shows the tubing fitted over the outflow post of the pump. Tubing can be purchased wherever you purchase your pump. You may also find it in gardening, craft, and hardware stores and in the aquarium section of larger pet stores. It is generally inexpensive and can be cut to any length with sharp scissors or a utility knife.

Tubing often comes with the pump. If not, or if you want to change the tubing for any reason, take the pump with you when shopping for tubing. The pumps do not state the required tubing size and you want to make sure it will fit.

Generally, the more narrow the tubing, the greater the water force, therefore the higher the stream; yet there is a greater water *flow* with larger tubing (the larger the tubing, the greater the flow). You can connect two sizes of tubing together by "telescoping" a series of gradually smaller sizes from the smallest to the largest, making the transition between the size from your pump and the size you wish it to be. There are also adapters which can bridge the seam between tubing of two different diameters, if needed (available at auto supply stores).

The tubing will travel from the pump up through the materials of your fountain's design until it reaches the point where you want the water to emerge. It should fit snugly through the hole in the fountain's material at this point. To make the tubing more manageable, the end of it can be warmed over a candle flame or in hot water. It will then be more pliable and easier to fit into this opening. Once the end of the tubing is inserted into the opening, the remaining tube pulls through more easily.

If you want to hide your tubing in a creative way, you can paint it to match your fountain filler material or even a special color to highlight a feature.

There are also tubing pipes and tubing elbows for situations where your tubing must bend or make its way through materials which might press too hard on it. These prevent crimping of the tube which would interrupt or reduce the flow of water.

PUMP HOUSINGS

You need to protect your pump from the heavy weight of rocks or other features. The item used to protect your pump is called a "pump housing." Literally it will be some kind of box or structure to "house" your pump.

Sometimes the housing for your pump is the same as one of the design features, such as an inverted clay pot or a bowl that is part of the overall design. Other times the pump will be protected with a housing that is purely functional and which will itself be covered from view. Examples of the latter are a plastic plumbing coupling, wire basket, pool drain, atrium drain grate, plastic plant basket, and homemade cages. These are just a few of the items that can be used for this purpose.

The housing must not prevent the water from reaching the pump, however. It must have openings that allow water to get it. If it is not already an open item, holes or openings must be cut at several points around it. An alternative is to raise it off the bottom, such as placing an inverted pot on "feet," so that water can flow under it to reach the pump. Some items that can be used for "feet" are galvanized corner brackets, plywood-spacer H-clips, glass marbles, or terra cotta feet. Make sure that all feet are the same height if the fountain design needs to be level.

The main considerations when choosing a housing are:
• Will it support the weight of the decorative materials that will rest on top of it?
• Is it a size that will cover the pump?
• Is it easy to cut or drill, if openings must be made in it?
• If not a decorative part of the design, can it be successfully hidden by other decorative materials?

One more function the pump housing serves (as a bonus) is to create a void space in the bottom of the fountain so that fewer rocks or other filler are required in the container.

CONTAINERS

*C*isterns, reservoirs, or basins as they are sometimes called are simply containers for the water and fountain pump. These are used at the base of your fountain. Sometimes they are the main design feature of the fountain.

Your container must be waterproof and deep enough to hold enough water to cover the pump. Most of the containers in this book are 2" to 5" deep. Your other considerations will be decorative, and the containers diameter or width will depend on where you plan to put it and what decorative items you plan to put in it.

There are suitable containers all around you, made of terra cotta, ceramic, stone, plastic, metal, concrete, and even a metal bucket. Pots, vases, and other containers can be found at garden shops and department or discount stores. You can also make your own containers from materials such as tiles from home improvement stores.

There are lovely containers that you might at first reject because they are not waterproof. Don't rule them out. You can waterproof them with sealants or liners. Look in garden shops for a plastic liner that would fit in the container. Also plastic bowls and other serving dishes from discount stores often make good liners and are inexpensive.

If desired, you can also paint your container to match your decor or to contribute to the mood of your fountain's design.

DESIGN FEATURES

The central part of each fountain contains a feature that attracts visual focus. Choosing this feature is very important, and this is where you can also give your imagination and artistic flair full rein.

Another term that is relevant here is "fountain head." This is the point of the fountain from which the water emerges. It is part of the design feature. The design feature also determines what happens to the water when it emerges – whether it cascades down flat stairs or pours into a receptacle on another level or follows some other action. This design element also helps make the fountain look as if the water is flowing naturally, and it will inform your remaining decisions for fillers and/or plants.

Practically anything can be used for a design feature, with only two requirements: 1) that it won't dissolve in water, and 2) that it can withstand the pressure of having a hole for the tubing drilled into it.

The photo will give you some ideas for central design features that can be used to make a fountain. You will find fountains in this book using some of these, and you can use your imagination to substitute or make your own. The size and shape are important. Choose a piece that is pleasing to look at. Try to imagine the vase or pot turned on its side or upside down. You may be able to scavenge your cupboards and find things that will work.

A marble piece or a tile structure can be your design feature. You may need to cut the tile or marble for your fountain. If you are adept at this skill, feel free to do it yourself. However, if you are unsure of your skill as a tile cutter, ask your local tile store or home building supply store to precut the tiles for you. They will usually do so at no extra charge, especially since you will only need a few tiles for most of these projects.

Rocks or slates that are piled atop one another for the water to cascade is another idea for a design feature. Breaking the rocks or slate to construct the design feature is less scientific and more fun. You *can* do this yourself. But you may need to buy a few extra so you can experiment until you get the size and shape you need. Stand on a stool and drop the slate or rock from this height onto concrete. This is best done outside without people (especially children) nearby. The small fragments you will get from this process can be used as filler, so don't throw anything away.

FILLER

Your fountain may call for materials to fill the container and conceal the pump, pump housing, tubing and cords. There are many natural and man-made materials that can be used. Your garden shop or home building supply store will have many of these shown here and more.

The nice thing about these fillers is their dual role – they display their own beauty, acting as wonderful accents, and conceal the mechanics of the pump at the same time. Consider the overall design and palette of your fountain. For instance, if your fountain is dark and sleek, consider black marbles or broken pieces of marble, black glass beads, or dark shiny rocks. If your fountain is light in hue, perhaps light colored broken shale, light ceramic tile, or seashells would be good. You can also be colorful and use many colored tiles or broken beach glass.

To be on the safe side, spread your chosen filler materials on a piece of plastic and give everything a coat of sealer before you use it. Porous rocks will particularly benefit from this protection.

Types of Filler

Slate

Slate has a lot of visual interest, and it can be broken into pieces from very small to large. For this reason, you can use it in two roles in your fountain. Larger pieces can be used as your design feature and smaller pieces can be used as part of your filler to add a unifying factor to your design. Paste wax rubbed on slate darkens it and makes the entire surface appear wet.

River Pebbles

The constant washing of pebbles by river currents rounds the edges of these stones. Their smooth surface has a calming effect, even visually, and they can bc waxed and polished for even greater sheen.

Marbles & Glass Gems

These glimmer like jewels, especially in water. You can use regular round marbles or flat half-marbles available in craft, floral supply and aquarium supply stores. These are very colorful and reflective. Colorful glass shards (with edges made smooth) are also available in these stores.

Stones & Rocks

Look for interesting and unusual stones and rocks at garden centers, gem shops, and aquarium shops as well as in your own yard. Features which make them particularly interesting are crystal formations and veins of a different color from the background. Remember that some rocks take on a special glimmer when wet; other's don't change their appearance. There are also finishing touches you can add. For instance, paste wax rubbed on black Mexican rocks makes the rocks a deeper black and shiny.

Shells

The ocean has always given us a myriad of treasures that are a decorative delight, whether just displayed on a shelf or used to make other beautiful items. Shells make interesting fillers for fountains as they are natural partners with water. There is a wide variety from which to choose.

PLANTS

O*ne* of the appeals of a fountain is that it lends an aura of fertility. Plants enhance this atmosphere even more, adding a lush look. A little green from a plant can also add a visual accent and a touch of color. Moisture-loving plants that are good for fountains are: bonsai, mosses, ferns, aquatics, and small house plants. Good examples of the latter are: Schefflera, miniature palms, nerve plants, baby tears, jade plants, and mimosa.

Types of Plants

Water Plants

Small aquatic plants are available at larger garden centers or where aquarium supplies are sold.

Air Plants

These plants do not need a lot of care. They need to be spritzed with a little water once a day. They do not need soil or water for their roots, but sunlight is necessary. The fact that they do not need soil is a plus for a fountain, as there is no soil to cloud your water or clog your pump filter.

Potted Plants

Plants can be potted in small terra cotta pots, then placed on rocks or marbles around the fountain. Beautiful hand-carved stone vessels are also available. You can add plant cuttings in these without worrying about dirtying the water.

SPECIAL EFFECTS

A fountain engages all our senses. Today this is especially true with a number of products that produce special effects to enhance the multi-sensory experience of a fountain.

Sound

The wonderful sound of moving water produced by your fountain can be enhanced with sounds of birds and breezes from nature CDs. Also, CDs playing flute or soft music can accompany the water sounds of your fountain. You may want to consider the proximity of your fountain to a secondary source for sound such as a stereo or a radio.

Water itself can make a variety of sounds. You must plan for the water sound you prefer when you design your fountain. Water can gurgle, bubble, trickle or make a rushing sound. The water flow setting on your pump can make a difference in the sound. Different types of rocks on which the water falls or flows can produce different sounds, as can the way the rocks are stacked.

Fog

Fog has a mesmerizing effect which can be quite pleasant as long as you don't have to drive in it. A fogger unit can be added to your fountain to create this nebulous beauty, like clouds around your fountain. Find foggers where you find the fountain pumps.

Candles

There are ways to create the fascinating combination of water and fire – elements which are usually antipathetic. Among fountain supplies, you can find beautiful hand-carved stone tealights and vessels to use in your fountain design. This is the way to add candlelight to your fountain with no wax spillage.

Light

Imagine the magical effect of a light shining through a rose-quartz stone beneath the water. You can create such effects by using submersible lights, available with fountain supplies. There are also submersible pump and light kits that include a transformer. The transformer converts the regular 120V current to a safer 9V current and allows the light to be fully submerged in water.

Also, light your fountain to its best advantage. If you have directional light from above, you can focus it on your fountain.

Scent

A few drops of a special scent can add an evergreen or herbal essence to your fountain. Add the scent to the water in your container. According to aromatherapists, various scents can also have chosen effects on your mood and general sense of well-being. These scents are available in discount stores, bath departments, and even craft stores.

SEALANTS

A variety of sealants and adhesives are used for several purposes in making a fountain. Some of these are sometimes used to both seal and adhere items at the same time.

The opening in the container through which the pump cord is threaded must be sealed to keep water from escaping. If a container such as terra cotta is not waterproof, it must be waterproofed to prevent seepage of water. If you have a doubt about the porous nature of your container, by all means seal it with a clear sealer. If you use porous filler materials or central design elements, they will need to be painted with a sealer, as well. Various elements of the fountain design are glued together to keep them permanently in position. The adhesives used must be water resistant lest the water destroy the bond and the glued pieces come apart.

Waterproofing products make many wonderful materials available to you for your fountain design that would not otherwise be usable.

Silicone Sealant can be used as a waterproof glue and can seal openings.

Flexible industrial strength adhesive (such as E6000 by *Eclectic Products, Inc.*): This flexible adhesive creates a strong and reliable bond for a wide variety of surfaces, including terra cotta, tile, concrete, metal, wood, fiberglass, glass, and plastic. It is also a sealant and can be used like silicone.

Epoxy Resin can be used to coat materials for the purpose of making them waterproof.

Epoxy is a two-part adhesive formula. When the parts are mixed together and applied to the surfaces to be adhered, it achieves a very strong bond.

Minimal Expanding Foam Sealant is used on one project to actually construct a "mini mountain" for the fountain design.

Plumber's Putty: This product can be used to seal an edge which abuts another surface when the results must be watertight.

Epoxy Grout or charcoal grout can be used to adhere and fill in between tile or slate pieces applied in a mosaic-like fashion.

DRILLS

If your chosen fountain design needs drilled holes, you will need to know how to do this without frustration or anxiety. Here are some basic tips to help you drill with confidence!

You need a drill that can accommodate varying speeds and hole sizes. There are different bits for different materials (such as a masonry bit for drilling through concrete). Talk to your friendly hardware store or building supply clerk to help you find the appropriate bit for your project. Bits come in different sizes. You should always have two or three sizes smaller than your final hole as well as the size of your final hole, as you will start drilling the hole small and gradually get larger.

Once you have marked your holes and are ready to drill, try a few practice runs before you drill on the real thing. The first hole that you make is called the "pilot hole" and should be two bit sizes smaller than

Diamond-Studded Drill Bit

Silicone Carbide Grinding Stone Bit

the final hole. Next drill a slightly larger hole in the same place. Then drill your final hole. Try to maintain the same drill speed and steady pressure for each hole drilled.

To drill on **ceramics, glass, rock, or seashells,** use a fast-speed mini drill and a 1/16" diamond studded drill bit . It is available at rock shops among other places. The drill bit needs to be cooled with water while drilling or the crushed diamonds on the tip of the drill bit will loosen and fall off. You can work under a slow-running faucet. It is best to start with a small hole, then ream out the sides of the hole to desired size. A silicone carbide grinding stone works well to ream out the sides of the hole.

To drill into **clear acrylic,** first make a pilot hole with a heated nail. Heat the sharp end of a nail over a candle flame. Press heated tip into acrylic to make a pilot hole. Place a piece of wood under acrylic. Drill hole using a 3/8" drill bit in a regular drill. Allow the drill bit to cut the acrylic instead of applying pressure to the drill. (Do not use a fast-speed drill or it may melt the acrylic.)

WATER

*W*ater is an obvious ingredient for your fountain, but there are a few things to consider:

• When you fill your fountain, the pump needs to be completely covered. If the pump runs dry, the motor of the pump will burn out.

• Water naturally evaporates, so be vigilant about the water level in your fountain before you turn it on each time.

• If your tap water is too acidic it may weaken the seals in your pump and cause damage. Test the pH level of your water. You can buy a pH kit at any pool supply and many home building supply stores. Your water should have a pH level between 5 and 9. If your water is extremely hard or has natural deposits of copper or iron, you may want to consider using bottled or filtered water.

• Your water needs to remain at a reasonable temperature. If your fountain is exposed to freezing temperatures, things will crack and break. Extreme heat from a radiator or other heat source is also not good for your fountain. It is best to keep water between 35 and 90 degrees.

• Keeping your water IN the fountain is another consideration. Leaks and drips on special carpets and linens will not increase the peaceful feeling the fountain is supposed to inspire. There are a number of sealants and coatings (discussed previously) that can help make the inside of a fountain leak and spill proof. Clear epoxy resin and other waterproof paint-on products can be found at hardware stores and home supply stores.

CONSTRUCTING
Your Fountain

Once you have designed your fountain and gathered all your materials, the construction will go quickly and easily. The containers and design features you have chosen will determine the complexity of the construction.

Step 1: Waterproof your container.

Not all base containers need to be waterproofed. If you are using a glazed ceramic dish, then most likely it will hold water without leaking or seeping. However, some containers such as terra cotta, over time, will seep water through. Metal containers may begin to leak around the seams.

Test your container. Place your container in a sink or bathtub. Fill it with water and let it sit for a minimum of 24 hours. Notice if there are any leaks or water seepage.

A plastic liner or bowl can solve some waterproofing problems. Other problems can be solved with silicone caulking or waterproofing products.

Step 2: Prepare your containers, housing, design features.

Most likely you may need to drill holes for tubing or cords in your vessels. See the "Drills" section in the MATERIALS chapter for more information on drilling.

Glue design feature items together if needed.

Prepare your housing so that it correctly accommodates the pump.

Step 3: Measure and cut plastic tubing.

Once you have decided on the point of water emergence, you can determine the length from this point to the pump outflow valve. Cut tubing to the size needed.

Step 4: Test your pump

Place your pump in the water container, attach the tubing, fill container with water, and test pump to make sure it works and is adjusted properly. Note where you have placed the dial. It is easier to test it before you have

constructed and glued your fountain. Once you are happy with this, you can begin the construction of your fountain.

Step 5: Construct your fountain

The design of the fountain will determine which steps are first in the construction. However, some basic steps need to be accomplished in the construction of any fountain.

- Place the pump in the base container.
- Secure the pump housing
- Attach the tubing to the pump outflow valve
- Place the design feature
- Thread the tubing through the holes in the design feature, or bring the tubing to the point of water emergence. Secure the tubing. In some instances, if your tubing goes through a hole in the design feature, you will need to seal around the hole with silicone caulking.

Step 6: Add plants or other special features (optional)

The kind of plants or special feature you add are left to your discretion. See the "Plants" and "Special Effects" sections in the MATERIALS chapter for more information.

Step 7: Add filler

Add rocks, marbles, shells, etc. to cover any of the mechanics of the fountain you wish to disguise.

Step 8: Fill base container with water

Now comes the fun part. Fill the base container with water. Dry off the area around the fountain and dry off the plug if you even think water has gotten near it. Plug the pump in and enjoy. ❑

Photo 1

Photo 2

This example of construction is the **Tile Tower** project.

Photo 1: The tubing is threaded through the holes drilled in the tower, which is the design feature in this fountain. Epoxy glue is used around the hole to seal and secure the tubing.

Photo 2: The tubing is attached to the outflow valve of the pump.

Photo 3: The pump adjustment dial is checked to make sure it hasn't been moved.

Photo 4: The pump is placed in the base container and the housing is checked and adjusted.

Photo 5: Potted plants are placed.

Photo 6: Filler is added to cover housing, plant pots, etc.

Photo 7: Base container is filled with water.

Photo 3

Photo 4

Photo 5

Photo 6

Photo 7

SAFETY

There are a few things we would like to mention here to keep everyone in good health. Follow these easy hints:

- Check your water level before turning on your pump. The pump should be covered with water. If you run your fountain without enough water, the pump will overheat and eventually burn itself out. This is often identified by a swelling of the casing that prevents the impeller from moving.

- Check your cord for kinks or snarls. Sometimes the effort to cover the cord will cause something too heavy to sit on the cord and cause a problem.

- Don't forget to put in a drip loop so that any water dripping down the cord goes on the floor and not into the electrical outlet. *Electricity and water don't mix.*

- Do NOT use an extension or homemade cord. The cords that come with the pumps are made with a special waterproof covering. Buy a pump with a cord that is long enough, or place your fountain closer to the outlet.

- Always dry your hands AND make sure you are not standing in water before you plug in your pump. Sometimes you can get a little wet when trying your pump's different pressure levels and getting the water level right. Don't be hasty and try to plug in your fountain without stopping and drying! *Electricity and water don't mix.*

- Never leave the house with your fountain running. It is an electrical appliance just like your stove and iron. Turn everything off if you plan to leave it unattended for any length of time.

- When drilling holes, always wear safety glasses or goggles. If you have the drill in your hand, you need something covering your eyes. This cannot be stressed enough. Even if you wear glasses you will need to protect them with shatter proof protective goggles.

MAINTENANCE

You want your fountain to last forever, of course, so follow these simple steps to make that happen. Well, it may not last Forever, but it will last much longer with good care and maintenance.

- Check your pump periodically to make sure no debris has clogged the intake filters. Sometimes plants or moss can clog the intake of water. A dirty filter will slow water flow and affect the execution of your whole creation.

- Your fountain may get a white ring around the inside from the mineral deposits left by the rocks, stones and water. This is especially true if hard water is used (and hard water should be changed more often). Clean the fountain with a cloth dipped in a citrus cleaner. There are also white scale cleaners sold where pumps and fountains are sold.

- Fountains can be prone to grow algae. You have created all of the perfect conditions for a science experiment. You can add special algae deterrent or a capful of hydrogen peroxide or bleach to your fountain water to keep algae from taking over. If you add this regularly, you will probably prevent this problem all together.

- You can take your fountain apart and clean the pump, making sure all the parts are free from debris and mineral deposit buildups. Most pumps will have a diagram of how to clean it and take it apart so keep those instructions around and follow them from time to time.

- And remember, one of the best ways to keep a fountain clean is to run it.

Tile Towers

Designed by Patty Cox

These beautiful white marble slabs remind us of ancient Italian fountains. The neutral color scheme adds to the tranquility of this look. The base container and tower design feature are constructed from marble tiles that are easy to find at home improvement centers.

Supplies

Pump: Submersible water pump

Tubing: Clear plastic 3/8" tubing

Container: Holding Tank & Base: Three 6" x 12" Rialto Italian tiles; two 6" x 6" square Rialto Italian tiles (available at home improvement stores; have tiles cut at the store at time of purchase as a wet circular saw is needed to cut ceramic tiles – see Step 1 of instructions); Copper metal sheeting, 5" x 7-1/4"

Design Feature: Tower: Three 6" x 12" Rialto Italian tiles

Housing: two 2" x 4" metal mounting brackets (found in hardware stores or lumber yards)

Filler: White marble rocks

Sealants: Epoxy glue and/or epoxy resin

Additional Hardware: Four metal corner bracket connectors

Tools: Spring clothespins; Drill and 3/8" drill bit; Optional wet circular saw to cut tiles, if you do not have them cut at the store when purchased

Fountain materials before assembly

Instructions

Assembly of tiles:

1. Ask the clerk at the home improvement ceramics counter to cut the 6" x 12" tiles to the following specifications. There is usually no charge for in-house tile cutting at the time of purchase.

   Top Tower (Fig. 1): Cut one 6" x 12" tile in half lengthwise.

   Center Holding Tank (Fig. 2): Cut 3/4" from the ends of two 6" x 12" tiles.

   Bottom Small Base (Fig. 3): Cut one 6" x 12" tile in half lengthwise. Cut 3" pieces off one end of each piece.

2. Assemble tiles with epoxy glue as shown in Fig. 6. Seal all joints and corners with epoxy glue or epoxy resin. I have glued corner brackets to the corners of the holding tank for extra stability.

3. Cut copper sheeting as shown in Fig. 4. Form copper pan as shown in Fig. 5. Drill a 3/8" center hole. Apply epoxy glue to pan sides, then insert pan into tower top as shown in Fig. 6. Hold in place with spring clothespins until glue dries.

Construction of Fountain:

4. Insert 3/8" tubing into pan center hole from tower bottom. Seal tubing to pan with a line of epoxy glue.

5. Arrange holding tank on small base.

6. Place mounting brackets in each side of holding tank to act as housing for the pump. They also become a base for the tower to rest on.

7. Attach tubing to pump.

8. Place pump between mounting brackets with tower resting on brackets. This is all shown in Fig. 7. The cord from the pump will rise over one side of the container. The back of the fountain can be placed against a wall to hide this or plants can be placed in back of the fountain as camouflage.

9. Add enough water to base container to cover pump.

10. Fill holding tank with white marble rocks. ❏

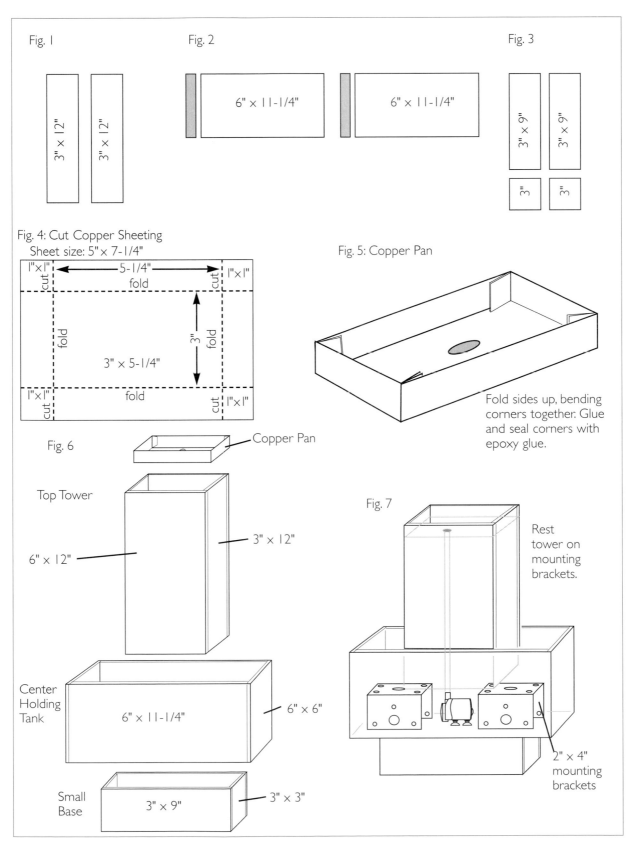

Fig. 1

3" x 12"   3" x 12"

Fig. 2

6" x 11-1/4"   6" x 11-1/4"

Fig. 3

3" x 9"   3" x 9"

3"   3"

Fig. 4: Cut Copper Sheeting
Sheet size: 5" x 7-1/4"

1"x1" cut   5-1/4" fold   cut 1"x1"

fold   3"   fold

3" x 5-1/4"

1"x1" cut   fold   cut 1"x1"

Fig. 5: Copper Pan

Fold sides up, bending corners together. Glue and seal corners with epoxy glue.

Fig. 6

Copper Pan

Top Tower

6" x 12"   3" x 12"

Center Holding Tank

6" x 11-1/4"   6" x 6"

Small Base

3" x 9"   3" x 3"

Fig. 7

Rest tower on mounting brackets.

2" x 4" mounting brackets

Slate Slabs Waterfall

Designed by Patty Cox

A rectangular ceramic container such as a planter or even a pasta baking dish can be the perfect size container to create a waterfall fountain. By simply stacking slabs of slate, a wonderful cascading effect can be created. The sound and sight are both mesmerizing and soothing.

Supplies

Pump: Submersible water pump

Tubing: Clear plastic 3/8" tubing

Pump Housing: Atrium drain grate, 4" (available at home improvement stores)

Container: Black ceramic glazed container, 9" x 13" x 3" deep

Design Features:
Two slate tiles, 11-7/8";
5 clear marbles

Filler: Aquarium gravel; 2 large and 3 small black Mexican beach pebbles

Plants: Sprigs of dried grasses or small plants of your choice (in small terra cotta pots)

Sealant: Two-part 5 minute epoxy glue

Tools: Utility knife; Drill and 1/4" and 3/8" masonry drill bits; Straight edge razor blade; Optional hammer

Fountain materials before assembly

Instructions

Pump Housing:

1. Cut a 1" section from a plastic bar on the side of atrium grate (Fig. 1), using a utility knife. Insert pump's electric cord through hole. Insert tubing through center top of grate.

Slate Slab Fountain:

2. The slate will need to be broken into 3 varying size pieces. The easiest method (though unpredictable) is to drop a slate tile from about 18" high onto a concrete sidewalk or driveway. The tile breaks into a few uneven sections. To create additional jagged edges, lightly tap a hammer on slate edges.

3. Select and stack three sections of slate. Drill a 3/8" hole through center of each (Fig. 2).

4. Refer to Fig. 2. Insert end of tubing onto pump outflow valve. Thread tubing through top of atrium grate and up through the hole of the largest slate piece. Press slate firmly to rest against grate top. Thread the second and third layers of slate onto tubing.

5. Refer to Fig. 2. Glue three clear glass marbles between the bottom and middle slate "shelves" as spacers. Glue two marbles between the middle and top slate "shelves."

6. Trim the tubing even with the top slate "shelf," using a straight edge razor blade.

Container:

7. Place the housed pump and slate "shelves" in the 9" x 13" ceramic base container. Fill container with water until pump is submerged. Adjust water flow dial to desired speed.

8. Place plants. Fill planter with aquarium gravel. Place a few black Mexican beach pebbles on gravel surface. Insert sprigs of dried grasses or other plants in gravel if using. ❏

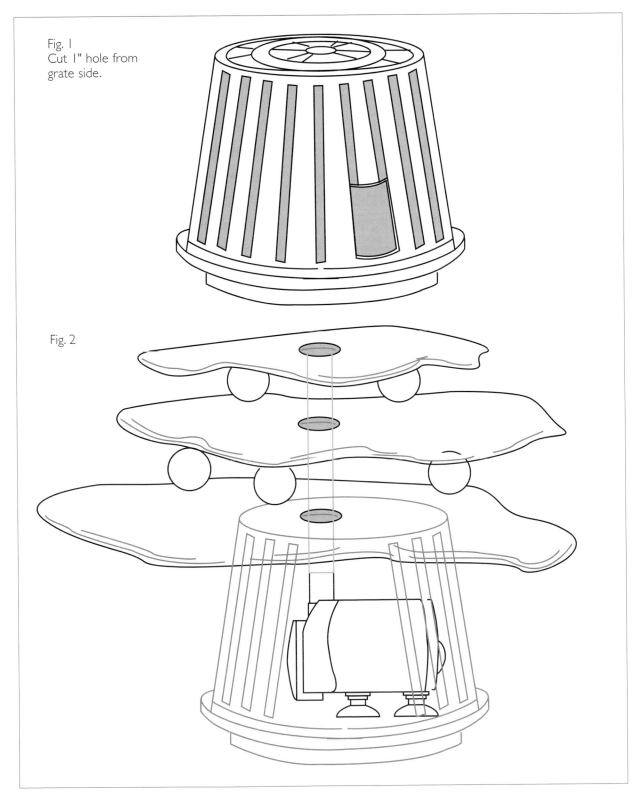

Fig. 1
Cut 1" hole from
grate side.

Fig. 2

Slate Mountain Falls

Designed by Patty Cox

This fountain looks like a Hawaiian volcano. Adding the little votive flower pot candles adds to the volcano's fiery ambience. Fire and water may not mix, but in this case, used together in this design they certainly create an exciting fountain. This fountain would be great as a centerpiece for an evening outdoor get-together with a tropical theme. Serve tropical fruit based drinks, grilled seafood with mango salsa, and you have got the makings of a great party.

Supplies

Pump: Submersible water pump

Tubing: Clear plastic 3/8" tubing

Pump Housing: Plastic plant container, 4"

Container: Ceramic planter saucer, 15-1/2" diam.

Design Feature:

"Mountain", made of minimal expanding foam sealant;

Aluminum foil;

Slate chips landscaping stones (pine mulch size);

Three small terra cotta plant pots, spray- painted black

Sealants: Flexible industrial strength adhesive;
Charcoal-colored mortar (or epoxy grout);
epoxy resin

Tools: Serrated kitchen knife

Plants: Air plants (optional)

Instructions

1. Cover the 15-1/2" plant saucer with aluminum foil. Place the 4" plastic plant container upside down along one side of the saucer with pump underneath planter (Fig. 1). Spray foam sealant in a ring around outer edge of saucer, incorporating planter in ring. *NOTE: Read all foam sealant label precautions. Wear protective gloves and work outdoors or in a well ventilated area.* Build up additional layers of the ring, making layers taller over the small planter (which will be the pump housing). Allow foam sealant to dry and cure for eight hours.

2. When cured, foam sealant can be easily cut with a serrated kitchen knife. Cut a hole through the top of mountain into plastic planter for inserting pump plastic tubing (Fig. 2). Cut another hole along outside back of ring to insert pump's cord. Carve a notch under the inverted planter for water return (Fig. 3).

3. Insert tubing on pump's outflow post. Pull cord through back opening.

4. With the serrated knife, cut 1/2" irregular stair steps all around the mountain (Fig. 2).

5. Glue slate chips on each stair step with flexible industrial adhesive (Fig. 4), as follows: Cut horizontal slits in the foam with a knife; apply the glue, then insert edges of slate chips in slits. Glue three small plant pots on foam ledges. Allow glue to dry.

6. Apply charcoal-colored grout on foam mountain, covering foam. Sponge grout off slate chips. Allow grout to dry.

7. Apply epoxy resin on all sides of fountain surface. This creates the shiny appearance. Allow resin to dry and cure.

8. Add water.

9. Place candles in small terra cotta pots. ❏

Top view of foam mountain assembly.

Front view with slate pieces added.

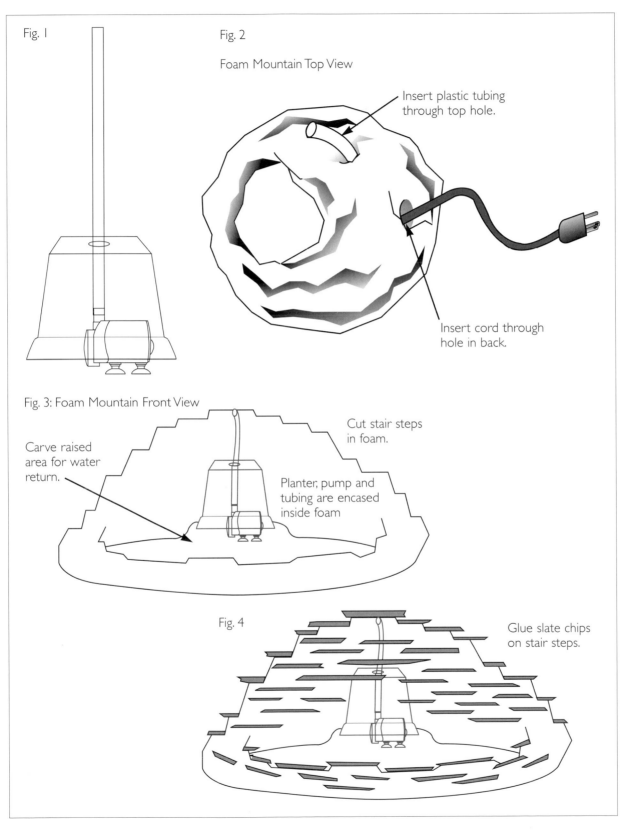

Fig. 1

Fig. 2

Foam Mountain Top View

Insert plastic tubing through top hole.

Insert cord through hole in back.

Fig. 3: Foam Mountain Front View

Carve raised area for water return.

Cut stair steps in foam.

Planter, pump and tubing are encased inside foam

Fig. 4

Glue slate chips on stair steps.

Concrete Tower

Designed by Patty Cox

The water gently trickles down the sides of this concrete tower. The rough texture of the concrete pillar with the silky-smooth water flowing down the side creates a contrast in textures that intriguing to the senses. The plants at the bottom of this pillar will thrive in their moist home. Although the pillar has to be constructed, the materials are easy to find and easy to use.

Supplies

Pump: Indoor/outdoor submersible water pump

Tubing: Plastic 3/8" tubing

Pump Housing: Square coated wire basket (such as a desk organizer), 5"

Container: Galvanized metal boat shaped container, 8" x 4"

Design Feature:
Pillar made with concrete mix or quick drying concrete mix;
2 quart empty milk carton;
cardboard toilet paper tube

Filler: stones

Plants: Baby tears and/or other plants that are potted in small terra cotta pots, plastic cracker bins, or small optional metal boat-shaped planters made with copper sheeting or galvanized metal to hold plants

Tools: Masking tape; Masonry shaper; Optional hammer

Fountain materials before assembly

Instructions

Making Pillar:

1. Open up the top of the milk carton. Cut a 3/8" hole in the center bottom of milk carton. Insert one end of the plastic tubing through this hole. (Fig. 1).

2. Measure 2-1/2" down from top fold in carton. Cut a 1-3/4" hole on two opposite sides of carton (exactly opposite each other). Insert toilet paper tube through holes (Figs. 1 and 2).

3. Secure top end of tubing near center of milk carton opening with an X of masking tape strapped to carton sides. The tubing inside the carton should curve around toilet paper roll, not touching sides of roll or carton (Fig. 1).

4. Pour concrete into milk carton. Allow to set at least 24 hours.

5. Remove milk carton and toilet paper tube. The concrete sides of tower will be smooth when removed from carton. To roughen surface, scrape sides with a masonry shaper.

Assembly of Fountain:

6. Turn tower over so that the peep hole in the pillar is near the bottom. Plastic tubing will be coming out the bottom of the pillar. Insert plastic tubing through a center space of the coated basket as in Fig. 3.

7. Place pump in container bottom and arrange basket and tower over pump (Fig. 3). Trim plastic tubing to correct length and place end of tubing onto outflow valve of pump. Trim top end of tubing even with tower top.

8. Fill base container with water until pump is submerged. Test pump at this time and adjust if necessary.

9. Pot plants in containers. A plastic cracker container works well as a mini planter. You can make small metal boat-shaped planters as follows: Cut copper sheets or galvanized metal to fit along the inside edge of your selected container. Fold bottom edge (Fig. 4). Fold each side end toward center twice (Fig. 5). Pound side fold flat with a hammer.

10. Place potted plants into base container, with plant pots resting on basket pump housing.

11. If needed, add filler stones around plants. ❏

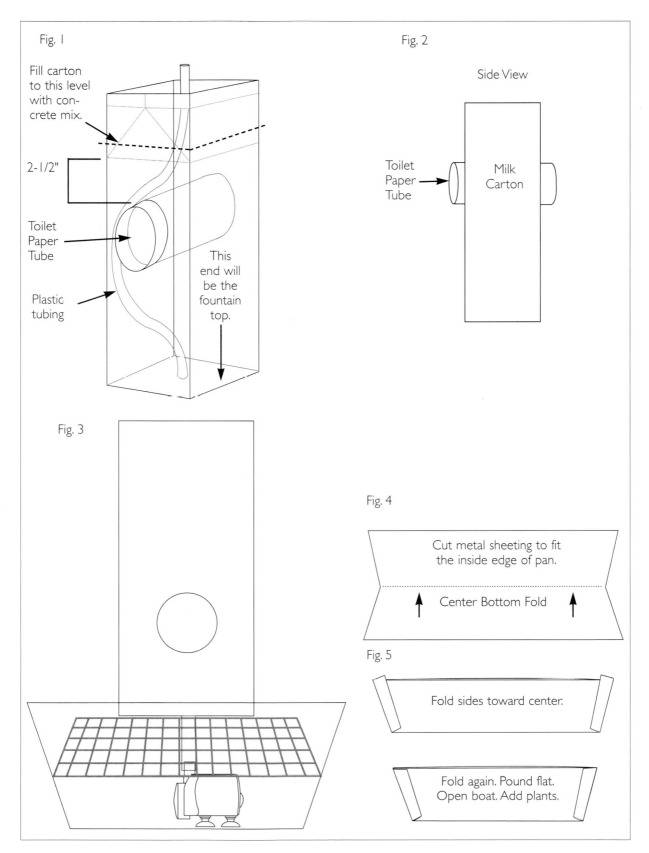

Fig. 1

Fill carton to this level with concrete mix.

2-1/2"

Toilet Paper Tube

Plastic tubing

This end will be the fountain top.

Fig. 2

Side View

Toilet Paper Tube

Milk Carton

Fig. 3

Fig. 4

Cut metal sheeting to fit the inside edge of pan.

Center Bottom Fold

Fig. 5

Fold sides toward center.

Fold again. Pound flat. Open boat. Add plants.

Schoolhouse Light

Designed by Patty Cox

This dome surely looks familiar to most of us. It is a light fixture dome that is most often used in institutional settings such as school classrooms. Light fixture domes and globes can make interesting design features in a fountain – and are inexpensive to purchase. Here a hole was already drilled in the center of the dome. This hole was conveniently used for the plastic tubing which carries the water to the emergence point. This design makes a compact fountain that has a quirky modern look. The pump can be adjusted to your preference – you can have the water spout up like a fountain, or you could have it simply gurgle up to the hole and gently flow down the sides of the globe.

Supplies

Pump: Submersible water pump

Tubing: Clear plastic 3/8" tubing

Pump Housing: Lath diamond metal mesh (from home improvement store); 24-gauge craft wire

Container: Black planter saucer, 16"

Design Feature: Ceiling light globe with predrilled center hole, 12"

Filler: Smooth black beach pebbles

Sealant: Flexible industrial strength adhesive

Tools: Tip snips or old scissors; Razor blade

Instructions

Pump Housing:

1. Cut a strip of metal mesh 3" wide. The length should be the circumference of the ceiling lamp base + 2" for overlap. Trace around the lamp base onto a piece of newspaper and cut out. Use this as a pattern to cut a metal mesh circle. Wire the 3" wide strip around the mesh circle as shown in Fig. 1, dropping the circle down about 1/4" from the edge of the mesh strip to create a lip. Overlap strip ends and wire together using craft wire.

Constructing the Lamp Globe Fountain:

2. Insert the 3/8" tubing through the center hole in globe (Fig. 2). (NOTE: If the tubing is not an exact fit, warm the tubing over a candle flame. The tubing can then be easily compressed to fit in hole and will stiffen again when cool.) Apply flexible industrial adhesive around tubing on the inside of globe to seal. When glue dries, cut excess tubing even with the outside of globe, using a razor blade. Cut the inside length of tubing even with the globe base.

3. Place pump in saucer container, centering the outflow post. Place wire mesh over pump. Cut a small hole in mesh to insert tubing, if needed and cut one on the side for the cord. Place globe on wire mesh, connecting tubing to outflow post on pump. Add water to saucer. Adjust water flow dial to desired speed.

4. Add black beach pebbles in saucer around lamp. ❏

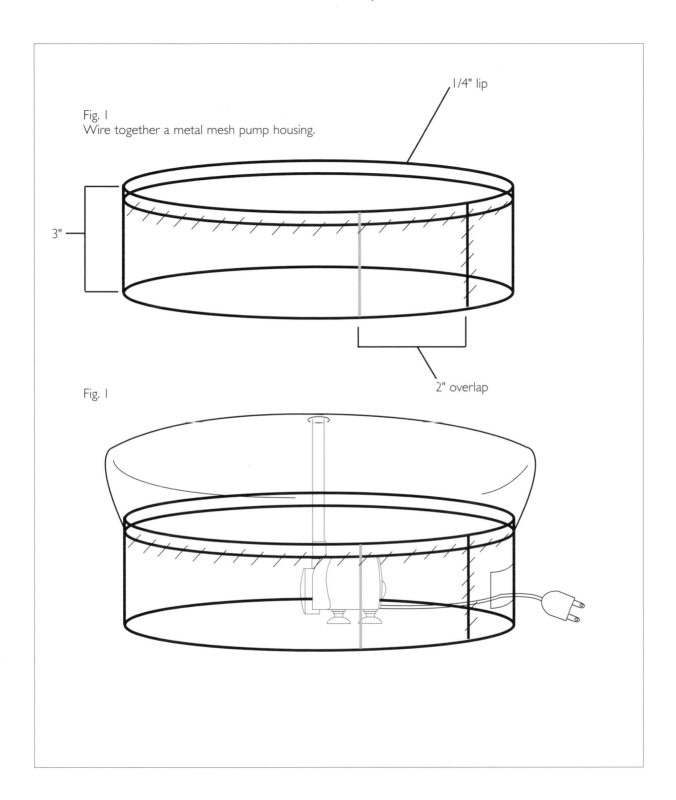

Fig. I
Wire together a metal mesh pump housing.

1/4" lip

3"

2" overlap

Fig. I

Global Meditation Table

Designed by Patty Cox

The sleekness of the finish on the containers and design feature, the globe-shaped forms, and the soothing running water all make this an exceptionally tranquil fountain. And the designer was exceptionally clever — who would believe that the top globe is a round salt shaker. The water pushes through the holes in the shaker, creating wonderful spouts of water. The spouting water fills up the first plate of stones, then cascades down the sides to the stone-filled base container. You can adjust the pump to your preference for the height of the water spout. All will be in harmony when this fountain is the focal point of an Oriental inspired space.

Supplies

Pump: Indoor submersible water pump

Tubing: 3/8" tubing

Pump Housing: Round shiny, black-glazed ceramic bowl, 5" diam.

Container: Black glazed ceramic square platter, 13" square

Design Feature: Black square plate, 8" (matches platter);Round salt shaker, 2-1/2" diam.

Hardware: Five H-clips (plywood spacers)

Filler: Black Mexican beach pebbles, large and small; Two bags black glass half marbles

Plants: Small potted plants, *(optional)*

Sealant: Epoxy glue

Tools: Mini drill with 1/16" diamond bit and silicone carbide grinding stone bit

Instructions

Pump Housing:

1. Drill a 3/8" hole in the center bottom of the 5" bowl.
2. Glue five H-clips (Fig. 1) around lip of bowl with epoxy glue (Fig. 2). This will lift the bowl off the base enough so that water can circulate.

Meditation Table:

3. Drill a 3/8" hole in center of the 8" square plate.
4. Glue plate on inverted bowl base, aligning holes (Fig. 2).
5. Thread tubing through housing and plate center holes. Arrange pump in bowl housing. Trim lower end of tubing to fit on pump. Detach tubing from pump.
6. Glue salt shaker over top end of tubing on plate table.

Platter Container:

7. Arrange pump in center (the deepest) portion of platter. Attach tubing to pump and place housing bowl over pump.
8. Fill platter with water.
9. Arrange rocks around plate-table and around bowl in platter.
10. *Optional:* Arrange potted plants on rocks. ❑

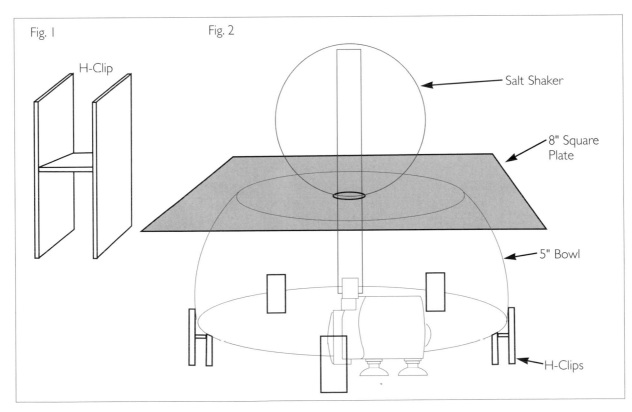

Agate & Figurine

Designed by Patty Cox

As water cascades down an agate slab and trickles onto rocks below, a faint tinkling sound soothes away your stress. And the angel figurine becomes a focal point for your meditation. A hole is drilled in the center of the agate slice so that the water emerges around the rocks placed on the slice and slides down the sides of the agate.

Any type of figurine can be placed in your fountain, giving it character and personality. A piece from a favorite collection can be shown off in this special place of honor. This design is especially adaptable to a variety of container sizes and statue types.

Supplies

Pump: Indoor submersible water pump

Tubing: Plastic tubing, 3/8"

Container: Oval gold planter, 7" x 10"

Design Feature:
Rust-colored agate slab, 5" (I used a predrilled clock face available at rock shops);
Figurine, 5" tall

Filler:
Small black Mexican beach pebbles;
Two pkgs. black marbles

Plants: Miniature fern or plant of your choice

Sealant: 5-minute epoxy glue

Tools: Razor blade

Instructions

1. Warm the end of plastic tubing over a candle flame. Insert tubing through center hole of agate slab (Fig. 1). Secure underside of agate slab to tubing with epoxy glue. If needed, a stabilizing rock can be glued between agate and pump. Trim top of tubing flush with top of slab, using a razor blade.

2. Place pump in center of vase. Place tubing on pump's outflow post, trimming tubing length as needed.

3. Fill vase with a mixture of black beach pebbles and black marbles. Place three beach pebbles around the top center opening of agate slab.

4. Place figurine on pebbles (Fig. 2). Arrange plant in pebbles. ❑

Fig. 1

Agate Slab

Optional
Stabilizing Rock

Fig. 2

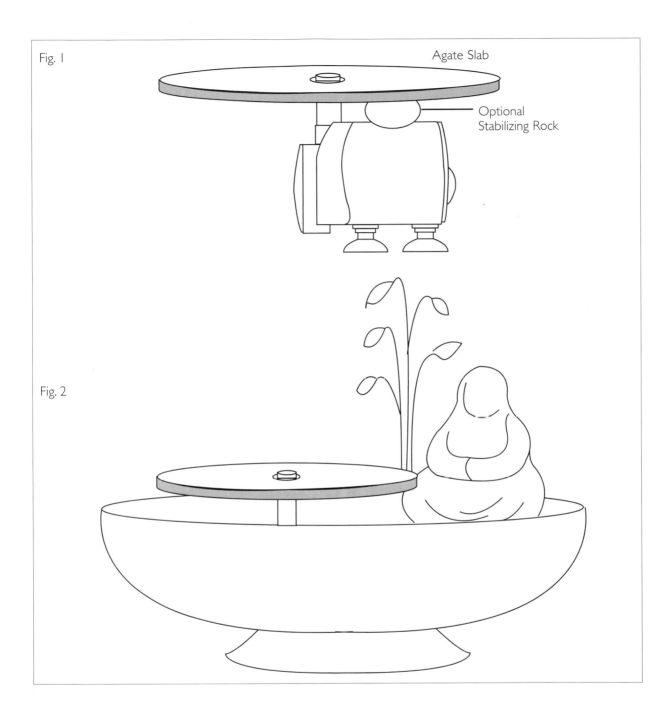

Stained Glass Lighted Fountain

Designed by Patty Cox

This fountain features a special lighting effect. The pump comes with its own light, so when placed inside this stained glass rectangle, it creates a warm glow. The "faux" stained glass globe was created with glass paint on an acrylic box. A pattern is given for the Frank Lloyd Wright-style design here; however any design can be created for this stained glass lamp fountain.

Supplies

Pump: Submersible water pump *with light*

Tubing: Clear plastic 3/8" tubing

Container: Black ceramic planter, 7" square x 2" deep

Design Feature:
Acrylic box, 4" square x 7" tall;
Instant faux lead lines;
Glass staining paints – amber, sunny yellow, orange, cocoa, brown, ruby, black

Hardware: Four 1-1/2" galvanized corner brackets

Filler: Black aquarium gravel

Sealant: Epoxy resin

Tools: Nail and candle; Drill and 3/8" drill bit; Glue stick; Straight edge razor blade; Toothpick; Optional steel wool

Instructions

Making Design Feature:

1. Remove and discard lid of acrylic box. Turn box upside down for fountain.

2. Hold the pointed end of a nail over a candle flame. Insert heated nail into center top (was previously bottom) of acrylic box. Use this hole as a pilot hole, then drill a 3/8" hole in same place to insert tubing.

3. Glue galvanized corner brackets at the bottom corners (open end) of box (Fig. 1). This will raise the box from the surface of the base container enough to allow the circulation of water.

4. Insert tubing through center hole of box from underside. Seal around hole and tubing with silicone caulking.

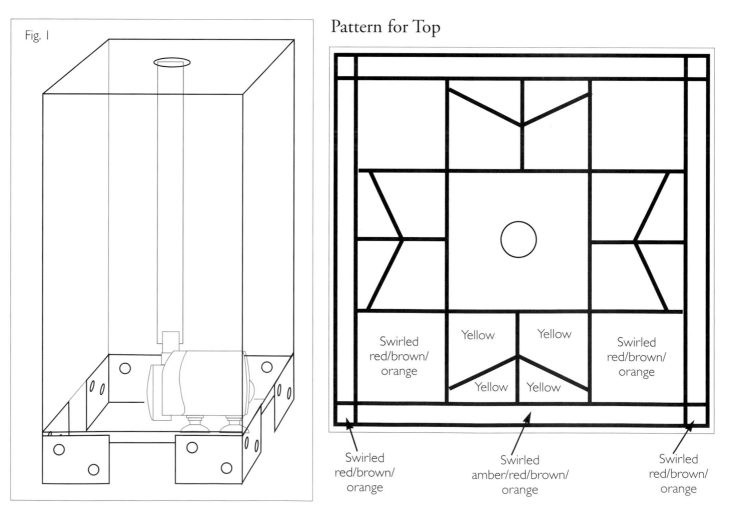

Fig. I

Pattern for Top

Swirled red/brown/orange

Yellow

Yellow

Swirled red/brown/orange

Yellow

Yellow

Swirled red/brown/orange

Swirled amber/red/brown/orange

Swirled red/brown/orange

5. Trace design pattern from book onto tracing paper; or make a photo copy of the pattern. Cut out the paper pattern of painted design and stick to inside of one surface of box.

6. Apply faux lead lines to outside of box, following lines of pattern. Remove pattern and adhere it to another side of box. Repeat. Continue applying faux lead to all sides of box and box top (use separate box top pattern for this).

Pattern for Sides

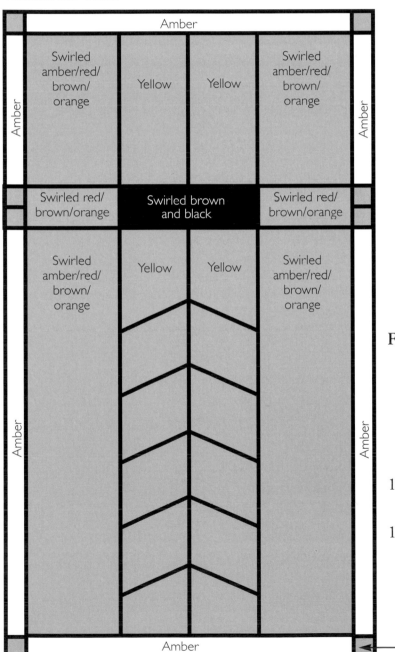

7. Following color indications on patterns; apply glass paints in all leaded sections. Swirl the multi-colored sections of paint with a toothpick. Allow each side of box to dry flat before painting another side.

8. When paint is dry, paint epoxy resin on top and sides of painted box. Allow resin to dry and cure. *Optional: For a frosted surface, dull the resin with steel wood.* This will seal the glass paints. Glass paints tend to get frosty and soft when they come in contact with water. Sealing the paints with resin will prevent this from happening.

Fountain Assembly:

9. Place pump under finished lamp-fountain. Measure and trim plastic tubing to the appropriate length and attach to pump. Trim top of tubing even with top of fountain, using a straight edge razor blade.

10. Add water to base container. Adjust pump's water flow dial to desired speed.

11. Fill container with black aquarium gravel. ❑

Copper Arch

Designed by Patty Cox

Water pours from the copper tubing, sliding down the sides of the slate slice and onto pebbles below. The pebbles sing as the drops of water splash against them, covering them with a beautiful wet gloss. For this fountain, the plastic tubing is inserted into the hollow copper tubing that has holes drilled at the bottom of the top piece. The hanging slate slice becomes the focal point of this fountain.

Supplies

Pump: Submersible water pump

Tubing: Clear plastic 3/8" tubing

Pump Housing: Wire mesh

Container: Ceramic planter, 4" x 9" x 2" deep

Design Feature: Arch made with a 24" length of 1/2" copper tubing (precut piece can be obtained at home improvement stores) and two 90-degree 1/2" copper pipe elbows; Slate slab, 4" x 5" (or agate slab); Copper strip, 6" x 1/2" (OR 18-24 gauge copper wire)

Hardware: Plastic suction cup, 1-3/4" (remove hook); 1/2" binding post rivet

Filler: Black aquarium gravel; Black Mexican beach pebbles – 2 lg. and 3 sm.

Sealant: Two-part 5-minute epoxy glue

Tools: Pipe cutter or hack saw; Drill and 1/16" carbide bit; 1/4" bit

Instructions

Copper Pipe Arch:

1. Cut the 24" length of copper tubing into three pieces as shown in Fig. 1 (5", 9", 7", discard 3").
2. Measure and drill five 1/16" holes along an even line on the center top 5" pipe (Fig. 2).
3. Connect pipe to copper elbows with epoxy glue.
4. Insert plastic tubing into shortest (7") side of pipe, fitting it snugly into first elbow joint. Trim end of tubing 1/4" longer than bottom of pipe.
5. Remove hanging hook from suction cup. Insert small front "nose" of suction cup into bottom opening of longest (9") pipe; this should be a snug fit.
6. Secure pump and suction cup in planter.
7. Place some wire mesh over pump to keep gravel away from pump intake valve.

Continued on next page

Slate Slab:

8. Break edges from a piece of slate, making an irregular-edge slab about 4" x 5". Drill a 1/4" hole in center top of slab.

9. Fold the 6" x 1/2" copper strip over arch. Punch a hole 1/2" from each end. Place copper strip ends over each side of slate where, aligning holes. Insert binding post rivet through holes. Screw rivet together to secure slate. (Optional: You can also use copper wire to secure slate to the arch.)

Container:

10. Fill container with water. Adjust water speed dial.

11. Remove some of the water, then add black aquarium gravel.

12. Stack black beach pebbles on the gravel. ❑

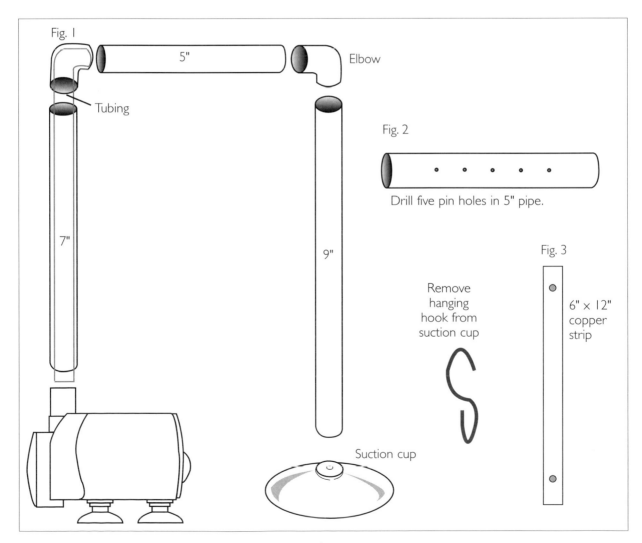

Fig. 1
5"
Elbow
Tubing

Fig. 2
Drill five pin holes in 5" pipe.

Fig. 3
Remove hanging hook from suction cup
6" x 12" copper strip

7"
9"
Suction cup

Copper & Beads

Designed by Rhonda Garson

Here copper again is used to create a metallic arch. This time strings of hanging beads are the vehicle for the streams of water. As the water comes from the holes in the copper tube, it flows down the strings of beads onto the rocks below. The tinkling of water with the movement of the beads creates an almost wind chime effect.

Supplies

Pump: Small submersible pump with outlet on top; 60 GPH @ 1 foot is more than enough performance. The 1/4" inside diameter copper tubing must fit over the pump's outflow post. Actually TRY the fit, don't just go by the specifications.

Tubing & Design Feature: Soft copper tubing with 1/4" inside diameter, straight 2 ft. length; Various sizes and shapes of glass and metallic beads; Five 3/16" metal washers for weight; 28 gauge brass beading wire for string beads, approx. 12 ft.

Container: Rectangular waterproof bowl, approx. 6-1/2" x 9" x 3", deep enough so that the pump will fit below rim

Filler: Several sizes of rocks (some should be rather flat, sizes should fit container); Small bag natural stone colored aquarium gravel; Florist's glass stones – red and gold or color you choose

Tools & Materials: Drill with 1/16" drill bit; Tape; Tubing Cutter; Sand or Salt, enough to fill the 2 ft. of copper tubing

Instructions

Placing Pump:

1. Place pump in the middle of the short side of the bowl with the outlet close to the wall. Position several medium sized rocks around pump to hold it in place and act as the housing. Run the electric cord where it will be the least visible. Set flow adjustment to medium setting. If that is too low or high, you can adjust it later.

Making Copper Arch:

2. Tape up one end of the 2 ft. soft copper tubing. Fill the tubing with either salt or sand. Tamp it down and refill making sure the sand or salt is tightly packed in the tubing. *This is to keep the tubing from crimping when you make the bends. This is a handy trick that the designer learned from her father.* Tape the other end shut.

Continued on page 70

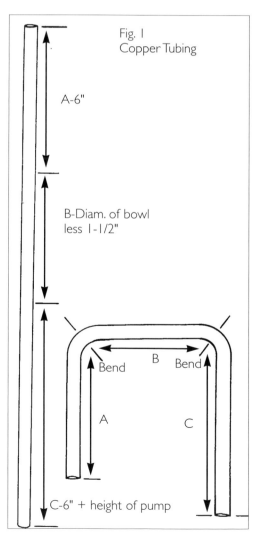

Fig. I
Copper Tubing

A-6"

B-Diam. of bowl less 1-1/2"

Bend   B   Bend

A

C

C-6" + height of pump

Instructions (cont.)

3. Refer to Fig. 1. Measure 6" from one end and make a mark for the position of your first bend. (Note: if your bowl is very deep and the top of the pump outlet is way below the rim, you will need to add the number of inches below rim to the 6" measurement. You want the horizontal part of the copper tubing approximately 6" above the rim of the bowl.) Measure the inside diameter of bowl. Subtract 1-1/2" from this dimension. This is the length for the horizontal portion of the pipe. For example, if bowl's inside dimension is 7-1/2", the horizontal portion of the pipe would be 6". Measure this distance from your first bend mark and make another mark for your second bend. Now mark where the pipe will be cut to length. Add the height of your pump to the measurement for your first bend. If your pump is 2-1/2" tall and your first bend is at 6", this last measurement will be 8-1/2". Measure down this distance from the mark you made for your second bend and make a mark. This is where the pipe will be cut after the bends are made.

4. Bend the copper tubing to a 90-degree angle at your first mark. It is best to bend the tubing around something like a knob on a cabinet or against the edge of a counter. Bend slowly to as close to 90-degree angle as you can. Make your second bend at the next mark. Your finished piece should look like an upside-down "U" with a flat top and one leg longer than the other.

5. Untape the ends of the tubing and empty out the salt or sand. Use a tubing cutter to cut your tubing to the proper length at the mark you made.

6. Measure the underside of the horizontal part of the tubing. Divide this measurement by five. This gives you the spacing for the four holes. Mark the position of the holes, making sure they are evenly spaced. Clamp or tape tubing down to a firm surface before drilling the holes. Drill the holes slowly and be sure not to go through the top of the tubing.

7. Check the height of the tubing by actually placing the shorter end over the pump outlet. The longer leg should be barely above the bottom of the bowl. If it is too long, cut some more off. If it is a bit shorter it will be okay – you can always place a stone or some gravel under the leg for support.

Adding Bead Strands:

8. Cut four 3-ft. lengths of 28 gauge wire – longer than you need, but you will trim it later. Thread one piece of wire into the first hole (closest to the short leg of the copper tubing). Feed this wire through the tubing and down the longer leg until it comes out the bottom of the tubing. Pull the wire until approximately 4" extends from the tubing. Repeat the same process with each hole, working in order from first to last. As you put more wire in the tube, the threading becomes more difficult, but be patient and they will all go through. It helps to hold the already threaded wires together and pull gently to one side of the tubing to keep them out of the way. After all of the wires are through the tubing, wrap all the ends (that come out of the tubing) together securely around a 3/16" washer and pull wires taut from the other ends. Now you are ready to bead on the ends of the wire that come from the holes in the copper tubing.

9. String beads on the wires in any order you like. You can mix and match or make them all the same. Finish each beaded wire with a 3/16" washer to add weight to the wire and help it hang straight. Wrap enough of the wire around the washer to secure it. Run the wire end back through the last bead for a finished look. Finished length of the wires, including the washer, should be 1/2" to 1-1/4" above rim of bowl. Beaded wires should be different lengths.

Assembly:

10. Place the short end of the tubing over the outlet on the pump. Position the larger rocks in the bowl (supporting the other end of the tubing, if necessary). Fill in with smaller rocks, aquarium gravel, and florist's glass stones. The area directly under the wires should be low enough for a small puddle of water to form when bowl is filled. This will help make a nice sound as the water drips off the wires.

11. Fill bowl with water to just below the rim. Plug in to see how the water flows out of the holes. If not enough water flows out of the holes, try restricting the flow out of the end of the tubing where the washer is by putting a small stone under the opening with tubing resting on it. You can also move the washer around or adjust the flow on your pump to change the flow rate. Adjust until you get the flow that works best for you. ❑

Yin & Yang Fountain

Instructions and photo follow on pages 72 & 73

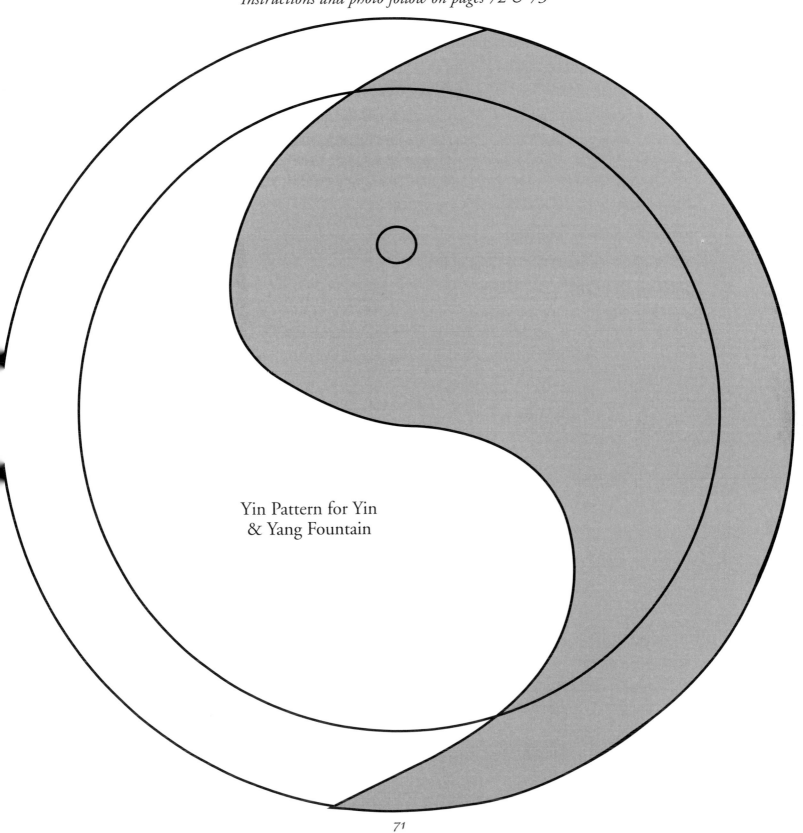

Yin Pattern for Yin
& Yang Fountain

Yin & Yang Fountain

Designed by Patty Cox

Moss and gravel are placed in the container to form the yin and yang pattern. Water gurgles up around the rocks to create a very subtle and tranquil fountain.

Supplies

Pump: Indoor submersible fountain pump

Container: Round black planter, 9" diam.

Design Feature/Filler:
Moss cloth (amphibian terrarium lining, available in pet departments/stores);
Natural aquarium gravel;
Three golden river rocks

Sealant: Silicone sealant

Tools: Mini drill and 1/16" diamond studded drill bit; Scissors

Instructions

1. With drill, carve a slot for the pump's cord in planter's side, working under a steady stream of water.
2. Place pump in planter with cord threaded through hole. Set the water speed dial at medium speed. Seal hole around cord with silicone sealant.
3. Fill planter with natural aquarium gravel.
4. Cut moss cloth using yin pattern. Lay larger end of moss over the pump. Cut a small hole through moss cloth at the pump's water outflow post. Tuck edges of moss under curved edges of planter.
5. Place three river rocks around water outflow post.
6. Fill planter with water. ❏

Pipe Dream Fountain

Designed by Rhonda Garson

This fountain couldn't be more simple. The materials are easy to find; and when assembled create a rustic fountain that is great for an outdoor area or a garden room.

Supplies

Pump: Small fountain submersible pump with outlet on top; 60 GPH @ 1 foot is more than enough performance

Tubing: Flexible plastic tubing to fit the outlet on your pump, 6" long

Container: Waterproof bowl, approx. 7-1/2" diam. and deep enough to cover pump (if using clay bowl, it must be sealed on inside to keep water from seeping through)

Design Feature: Copper pipe, 6-1/2" long, 3/4" inside diam. (tubing must fit inside pipe)

Filler: Several sizes of rocks (some should be rather flat, sizes should fit container)

Plants: Your choice; miniature ferns work well to give a nice backdrop of green behind the bright copper center tube.

Instructions

1. Place pump in the center of the bowl. Position several medium sized rocks around the pump to hold it in place and act as the housing. Run your electric cord so it will be in the least visible position.

2. Place the plastic tubing over the outflow valve of the pump.

3. Stack rocks around the pump, filling the bowl to the top of the pump. It is not necessary to pack the rocks in tightly. Once the rocks are to the top of the pump, place the copper pipe over the plastic tubing.

4. Stack the flatter rocks around the copper pipe in a spiral design. Layer rocks from largest to smallest. Leave approximately 4" of the pipe exposed above the top layer of rocks.

5. Fill the bowl with water. Be sure the pump is fully submerged. If your pump has a flow adjustment, start with it in the medium setting. If that is too low or too high, remove rocks as needed to access the flow control, make your adjustment, then replace the rocks. ❑

Abalone Enchantment

Designed by Patty Cox

Water spills from the center of the abalone shell and falls onto white marble rocks. The look is so luminescent with the pearly shell and the sparkling water on the translucent marble rocks. Little wire dragonflies flutter around this inviting scene. The dragonflies can be easily made using aluminum wire. This fountain would be equally as intriguing without the dragonflies.

Supplies

Pump: Indoor submersible water pump

Tubing: Clear plastic tubing, 5" length

Pump Housing: Clear acrylic bowl, 5-1/2" diam. x 3-1/2" deep

Container: Shallow green bowl planter, 10-1/2" diam.

Design Feature: Abalone shell, 6" high;

Optional: Two abalone beaded & wire dragonflies (instructions follow fountain instructions)

Filler: White marble rocks; Clear iridescent half marbles

Sealants: Flexible industrial strength adhesive (such as E6000 by *Eclectic Products, Inc.*); 5-minute epoxy glue; White epoxy mortar

Tools: Mini drill tool and diamond coated drill bit; Drill and 3/8" and 1/4" carbide drill bits

Instructions

Pump Housing:

1. Drill a 3/8" hole in center bottom of acrylic bowl.
2. Drill holes around bowl sides 1/2" from lip of bowl (see Fig. 1).
3. Drill or cut a hole in one side of bowl to insert plug (see Fig. 1).

Shell:

4. Drill a 3/8" hole in large end of shell, using a mini drill and diamond bit.
5. Align hole of shell with center hole in bowl. Glue shell and bowl together with epoxy

Continued on page 78

Instructions (cont.)

glue. See Fig. 2.

6. Thread a 5" length of clear plastic tubing through holes (Fig. 2). TIP: soften tubing over a candle flame for easier threading.

7. Arrange and adhere white marble rocks on bowl sides with flexible industrial adhesive, leaving drilled holes in bowl uncovered. Let dry. Apply white epoxy mortar between rocks. Let dry.

8. Place pump under bowl. Cut tubing to correct length. Fit tubing on pump outflow post.

Container:

9. Arrange pump and bowl with shell in green planter. *Optional: Place wire dragonflies in planter – see instructions for making them.* Fill area around bowl with additional white marble rocks. Sprinkle iridescent marbles over rocks.

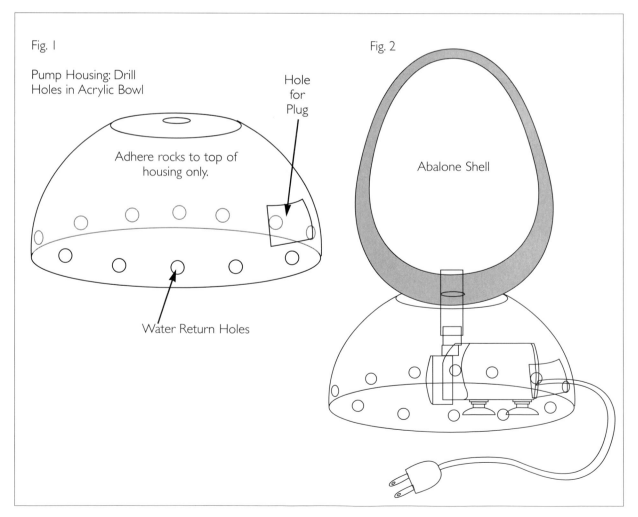

Fig. 1

Pump Housing: Drill
Holes in Acrylic Bowl

Hole
for
Plug

Adhere rocks to top of
housing only.

Water Return Holes

Fig. 2

Abalone Shell

Bead & Wire Dragonflies

Supplies

16 gauge aluminum buss wire, 24" length

22 gauge silver wire, 24" length

Five abalone beads per dragonfly

Needlenose pliers

Instructions

1. Cut a 24" length of buss wire. Grasp wire end with needlenose pliers. Form a coil for head as shown in Fig. 1.
2. Make a 1-1/2" loop around a pencil. Make three more 1-1/2" loops, forming wings back and forth in a figure-8 pattern. (Fig. 1).
3. Bend wire down to make a 6" to 8" tall stand (Fig. 1). Coil the bottom end.
4. Wrap wing centers together with 22 gauge wire, leaving a tail (Fig. 2).
5. Add five abalone beads on tail wire. Trim wire to 1". Bend wire end into a small loop to secure beads. ❑

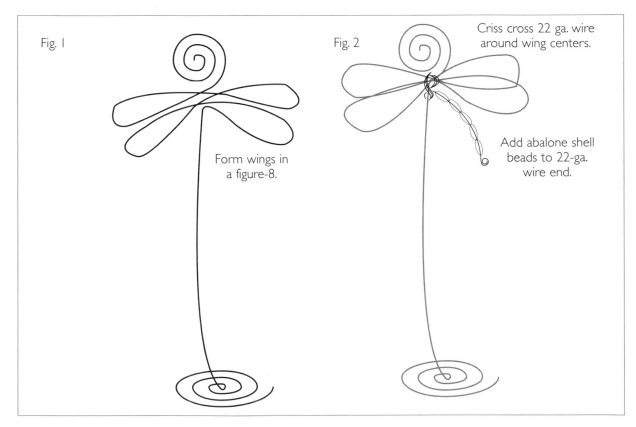

Fig. 1

Form wings in a figure-8.

Fig. 2

Criss cross 22 ga. wire around wing centers.

Add abalone shell beads to 22-ga. wire end.

Sea Treasures

Designed by Patty Cox

Seashells are so alluring, and they are the perfect design element to combine with flowing water. Here a large seashell planter is the base container. Water spouts up from a smaller seashell that is resting on a bed of pearlescent glass gems. This unit looks like a glistening treasure chest of water jewels. This fountain is one of the easiest and most alluring to make.

Supplies

Pump: Indoor submersible water pump

Tubing: Clear plastic tubing

Container/Design Feature: 9" ceramic or plaster conch shell vase (if you can find a large enough "real" shell then it would work fine)

Design Feature: Two sea urchin shells; Sand dollar

Filler: White aquarium gravel; Pearlescent half marbles

Plants: Dried grasses

Sealants: Flexible industrial strength adhesive; Clear epoxy resin; silicone adhesive/caulking

Tools: Drill and 1/4" carbide drill bit; Old paintbrush

Miscellaneous: Duct tape; Plaster of Paris (if you are using a plaster shell); White enamel spray paint (if you are using a plaster shell)

Instructions

1. If you are using a shell that is plaster, it will need to be coated inside with resin finish and spray painted outside with white enamel spray paint to make it water tight. If you are using a glazed ceramic shell, then it probably will not leak water. If you can find a large enough real shell, then this can be used also with no preparation.

2. Drill a hole in back of shell (above the water level) for pump's cord (see Figs. 1 and 2). (NOTE: Shell vase used is made of plaster; holes are easily drilled with a drill bit).

3. Place pump in vase with plug coming through hole. Adhere duct tape on inside of shell at hole. Patch area around plug with Plaster of Paris if you are using a plaster shell (Fig. 2) or silicone caulking if you are using a ceramic shell or a real shell. Let dry. Remove duct tape.

4. *For plaster shells only:* Lightly sand patched area. Touch up paint the patched area.

5. Place tubing on pump. Fill vase with a mixture of white aquarium gravel and pink half marbles. Trim plastic tubing to about 1" above gravel level.

6. Glue a sea urchin over tubing, leaving center hole open. Place another sea urchin on gravel. Insert a sand dollar and dried grasses in gravel as shown in photo of project. ❑

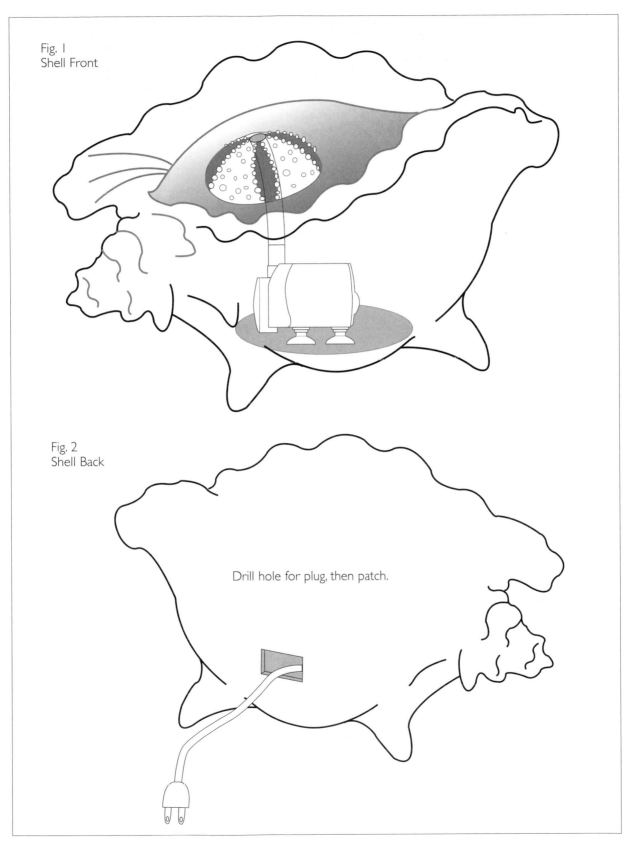

Fig. 1
Shell Front

Fig. 2
Shell Back

Drill hole for plug, then patch.

Copper & Wind Chimes

Designed by Kathi Bailey

This fountain gives two wonderfully soothing sounds; running water and tinkling chimes. Place this fountain where a breeze can gently rustle the chimes. Copper tubing is shaped into a serpentine design and plastic tubing is inserted to carry the water to the emergent point at the end of the copper tubing. The water splashes on rocks creating a gentle tinkle.

Supplies

Pump: Mini statuary fountain pump, 90 GPH

Tubing: Clear vinyl tubing, 1/4" diam., 2-1/2 ft. length

Pump Housing: Two or three flat flagstones; Several rocks about the height of pump

Container: Ceramic bowl, 9" diam. x at least 4" deep

Design Feature: Soft copper tubing, 1/4" diam, 18" length; Pkg. copper wind chimes; Fishing line, 1 ft. length

Filler: Assorted smooth river rocks, 1/2 lb.

Plants: Optional moss.

Sealant: Silicone adhesive or Flexible industrial strength adhesive

Tools: Metal cutting saw; Scissors

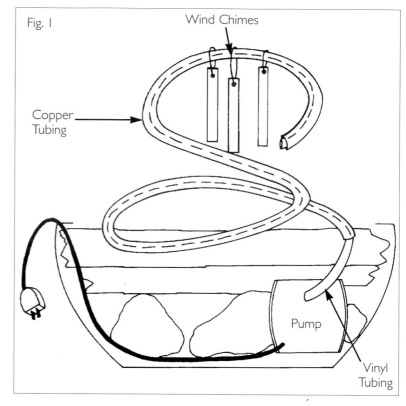

Fig. I — Wind Chimes — Copper Tubing — Pump — Vinyl Tubing

Instructions

1. If copper tubing has not been cut to length, use a metal cutting saw to cut an 18" length. Insert vinyl tubing through the copper tubing, keeping excess at bottom end.

2. Use your hands to slightly and slowly curve copper tubing into 2-1/2 large swirls, keeping bottom swirl almost flat, as shown in Fig. 1. Do not *kink* tubing, as that would interfere with water flow. **Test pump and water flow through tubing before completing your fountain. If flow is not strong enough, you may need to decrease length of copper tubing, then vinyl tubing.**

3. Attach bottom end of vinyl tubing to pump and place pump at bottom of bowl. Add flat stones to cover pump and lower end of vinyl tubing. (NOTE: If you need to place some stones the height of pump under the flat stones beside the pump to support the flat stones, do so – see Fig. 1.)

4. Add river rocks and optional moss on top of flat stones.

5. Cut fishing line into three 4" lengths. Insert into three wind chimes and knot. Glue to top of copper swirl.

6. Add water to bowl. Plug in pump and adjust water flow as needed. ❏

Fountain Rain on Glass

Instructions and photo follow on pages 88-89

Tulip Stencil Pattern
Transfer to Stencil Material and cut out design openings.

Fountain Rain on Glass

Designed by Kathi Bailey

Water streams down this piece of etched glass, creating the look of ran on a window. Dream away your afternoon watching crystalline water trickle down the clear etched glass.

Supplies

Pump: Mini statuary fountain pump, 120 GPH

Tubing: Clear vinyl tubing, 1/4" diam., 2 ft. length

Pump Housing: Plastic foam rectangle, 8" x 6" (large enough to fit snugly at sides into rectangular bowl)

Container: Rectangular ceramic bowl, 10" x 6" x at least 6" deep

Design Feature: 8" x 10" metal picture frame with glass insert; Blank stencil material, 8" x 10" (for etched design); Stencil adhesive spray; Glass etching medium (to etch flower on glass)

Hardware: Water flow stopper to fit vinyl tubing

Filler: Assorted glass beads and black glass stones, 1/2 lb.

Sealant: Silicone adhesive or flexible industrial strength adhesive

Tools: Craft or utility knife; Paint brush; Large needle

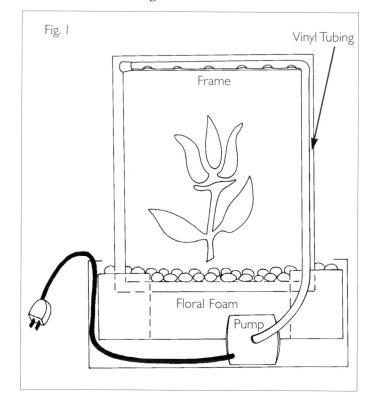

Fig. 1 — Vinyl Tubing, Frame, Floral Foam, Pump

Instructions

1. Remove backing from picture frame and glue glass into frame. Let dry. Clean glass with window cleaner before continuing.

2. Trace tulip pattern onto stencil material. Cut out stencil with craft or utility knife. Spray back of stencil with stencil adhesive and place on front of glass. Make sure edges of cutout areas are adhered to glass to prevent bleed under. Following manufacturer's instructions, apply glass etching medium. Remove stencil and let dry completely.

3. Attach water stopper to one end of vinyl tubing. Glue tubing to upper back of frame so that tube slightly overlaps onto glass, and glue tubing down one side. Let dry overnight to ensure bonding.

4. Poke six to eight small holes in tubing across the top. Keep holes as close to glass as possible so that water will flow down glass, not spurt out from back. DO NOT create holes on tubing that goes down the side. **Test the water flow before completing fountain.**

5. Cut a 4" piece of foam from back of large block. Insert foam tightly into rectangular bowl. See Fig. 1. Attach bottom end of tubing onto pump and place pump through the cutout opening in foam into bottom of bowl.

6. Insert bottom of frame approximately 1" down into foam so that it is lodged securely. Use silicone adhesive to secure it. Allow to dry.

7. Add glass beads and black stones on top of foam.

8. Add water, making sure that pump is submerged.

9. Plug in pump and adjust water flow at back. ❑

Embossed Shell Delight

Designed by Patty Cox

This fountain would be perfect for a bathroom or a room where a seaside design theme is used. Its sleekness and shell motif seem to suggest the look found in many bathrooms. This center design feature with the shell motif is easy to construct from tiles that you can find in most home improvement centers. Water gurgles up through this tower filled with pearly glass marbles that give the appearance of bubbles. As the water spouts, it spills over the sides of the tower into the base container to recirculate. A variety of base containers could be used for this as long as they are deep enough to hold the pump.

Supplies

Pump: Submersible water pump

Tubing: Clear plastic 3/8" tubing

Design Feature: Acrylic box photo frame, 4" x 6"; Two 4" square ceramic tiles embossed with shell design (available at home improvement stores); Two 2" x 6" edging tiles

Container: Rectangular ceramic vase, 9" x 7" x 3" deep

Filler: Clear half marbles; White aquarium gravel or rocks

Sealants: Tile adhesive; 2-part epoxy glue

Tools: Drill and 3/8" drill bit; Nail and candle

Instructions

Making Design Feature:

1. Remove and discard the cardboard insert in acrylic box frame. Measure and mark a dot in the center of one short end of frame. Heat the sharp end of nail over a candle flame. Press heated tip into acrylic, making a pilot hole. Place a piece of wood under acrylic. Drill hole, using a 3/8" bit in drill (Fig. 1).

2. Draw a pencil line 3/4" from top on the back of all the ceramic tile pieces.

3. Mix epoxy glue.

4. Glue the tile pieces onto the frame sides, aligning the 3/4" mark with the top of the frame. (Fig. 2). The top 3/4" of tiles will form a ceramic pool for the water at fountain top. Optional: Fill in small spaces between tiles with white tile adhesive, using it like mortar. Let dry.

Assembling Fountain:

5. Warm the end of plastic tubing for easier manageability, then insert end of tubing through hole in acrylic frame from inside.

6. Place pump on bottom of box frame. Trim lower end of plastic tubing, then attach it to pump's outflow post (Fig. 3).

7. Place pump and frame into shallow vase. Pour water in vase, covering pump. Adjust water flow dial. Remove some of the water, if needed.

8. Add marbles and rocks in base container. Put marbles into top pool of tile tower. ❏

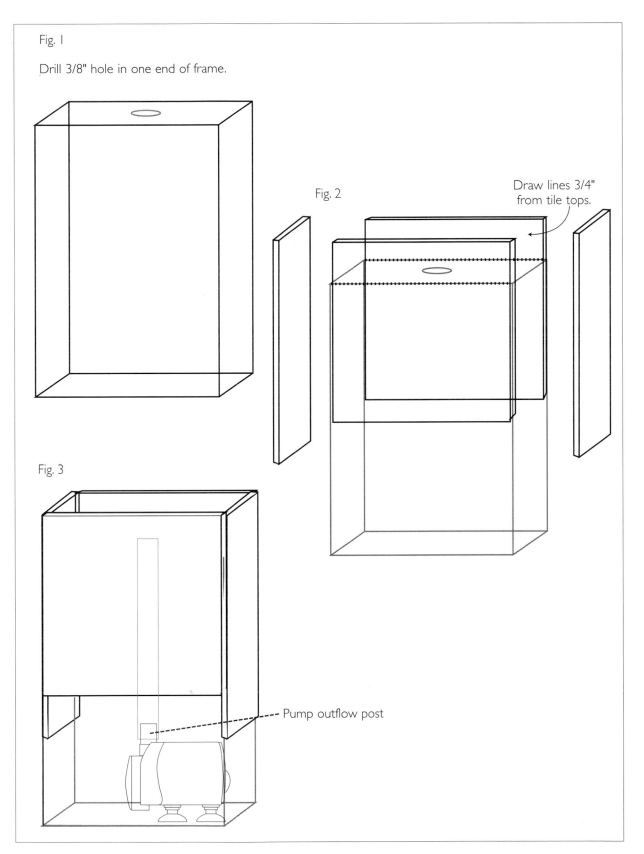

Fig. I

Drill 3/8" hole in one end of frame.

Fig. 2

Draw lines 3/4" from tile tops.

Fig. 3

Pump outflow post

Hurricane Globe & Shells

Designed by Rhonda Garson

We can't help ourselves from picking up shells at the beach and bringing them home. Then what do we do with them? This is the perfect place to show off your shell collection. This fountain features a clear glass hurricane lamp globe filled with shells. A variety of glass containers would work as long as you could drill a hole into the bottom for the glass tubing – hurricane globes are open at both ends so there is no problem with inserting the tubing.

Supplies

Pump: Small fountain submersible pump with outlet on top; 60 GPH @ 1 foot is more than enough performance

Tubing: Flexible plastic tubing to fit the outlet on your pump, 10" long

Container: Waterproof bowl, approx. 7" diam. and deep enough for you to cover pump (if using clay bowl, it must be sealed on inside to keep water from seeping through)

Design Feature: Glass hurricane lamp globe, 10" tall

Filler: Lots of shells, different shapes and sizes; A few medium size stones to hold pump in place in bowl

Optional: Resin finish for sealing inside of bowl

Instructions

1. Place pump in the center of bowl. Position several medium sized rocks around pump to hold it in place. Run your electric cord out of the bowl where it will be in the least visible position.

2. Attach one end of the plastic tubing to the outflow post of the pump. Bring the plastic tubing up through the hurricane glove and rest the globe on the rocks above of the pump. Cut the tubing so that it is 1" below the height of the hurricane globe. You might want to tape the tubing in place to top of globe to hold it temporarily while you fill the areas with shells.

3. Fill the hurricane globe with shells, keeping the plastic tubing in the center of the globe. (If you have taped tubing in place, remove tape before filling globe with shells.

4. Fill the bowl with water. Be sure the pump is fully submerged. If your pump has a flow adjustment, start with it in the medium setting. If that is too low or too high, adjust as desired. You will want to have it adjusted so that the spout is high enough coming out of the globe to be seen. Water does not have to go over the outside of the globe; it looks great gurgling up and flowing along the inside of the globe. But this is up to you, you can adjust it so that the spout goes high enough to push some water over the outside of the globe.

5. Place shells around the pump, filling the bowl to the top of the pump. It is not necessary to pack shells in tightly. ❑

Terra Cotta Tiers

Designed by Patty Cox

Simple and inexpensive terra cotta pots and saucers of varying sizes make exceptionally nice fountains. They are very easy to assemble and maintain. And your imagination is the limit when it comes to size. Just as long the proportion of the saucers and pots works, then your fountain can be tiny – made with 2" and 3" pots; or larger – made with 6" and 8" pots with appropriate sized saucers. When making a larger fountain, be sure to buy a pump that will push the water high enough for your size fountain. Mossy plants or fern work well in this fountain.

Supplies

Pump: Outdoor submersible water pump

Tubing: Clear plastic 3/8" tubing

Design Feature: Two terra Cotta plant pots, 4" and 3"

Container:
Three terra cotta plant saucers, 11", 8" and 4";
Three terra cotta planter feet (Fig. 1)

Filler: River stones

Sealants:
Flexible industrial strength adhesive;
Silicone caulking;
Epoxy resin

Tools: Mini drill and silicone carbide grinding stone bit

Instructions

1. Waterproof the inside of the largest terra cotta saucer with epoxy resin. Allow to dry and cure. This is the only one that needs to be water-tight.

2. Ream out the holes in the bottom of the 4" and 3" pots, if needed, to 3/8" diameter so that tubing can go through the holes. Use a mini drill with grinding stone bit.

3. Drill 3/8" holes in centers of 4" and 8" saucers to accommodate tubing.

4. The 4" pot at the bottom is the pump housing. Turn it upside down and glue the 8" saucer centered on top, aligning holes. Glue the 4" saucer on top of inverted 3" pot, aligning holes. See Fig. 2

5. Push the plastic tubing through the 4" pot and saucer, then through the 3" pot and saucer. Trim tubing evenly with surface on top of 4" saucer. See Fig. 3. Use silicone caulking around the hole in the top saucer to seal the hole and to secure the tubing.

6. Place the pump in the 11" saucer as shown in Fig. 3. Secure tubing on pump's outflow post, trimming length of tubing as needed.

7. Place the housing pot (4" pot) over the pump on the terra cotta feet.

8. Add water to the 11" saucer. Adjust water flow speed.

9. Fill all three saucers with river stones. ❏

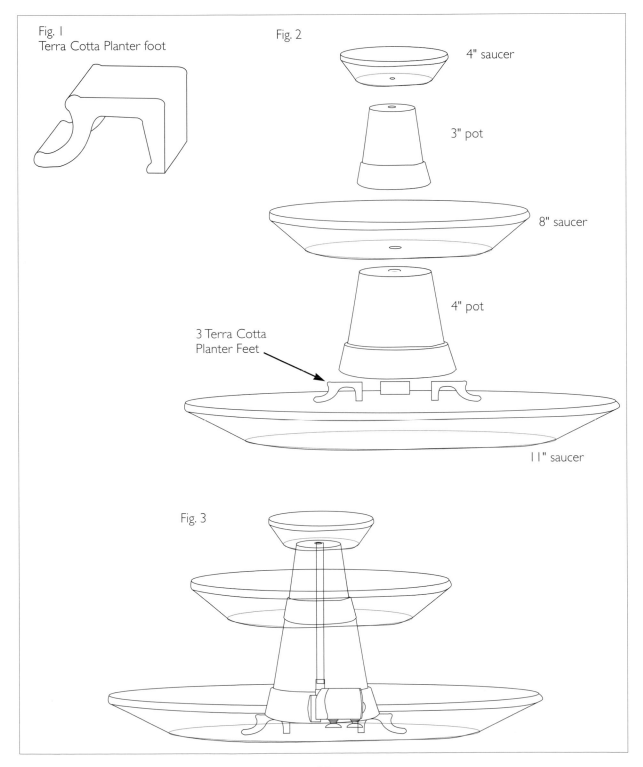

Fig. 1
Terra Cotta Planter foot

Fig. 2

4" saucer

3" pot

8" saucer

4" pot

3 Terra Cotta
Planter Feet

11" saucer

Fig. 3

Double Beauty

Designed by Rhonda Garson

This rustic fountain would make a nice patio, porch, or sunroom fountain — or bring this outdoor look inside to the kitchen or family room. It has an earthy attractiveness that evokes an image of a country French chateau. Mossy plants work well for this look.

Supplies

Pump: Small fountain submersible pump with outlet on top; 60 GPH @ 1 foot is more than enough performance

Tubing: Flexible plastic tubing to fit the largest outlet on your pump, 12" length

Pump Housing: Two pieces of plastic foam (NOT florist's foam!), any color, 12" square x 1/2" - 1" thick. This will be used to create a space for the pump.

Container: Round clay pot with no drain hole, 10" diam. x 7" deep (inside must be sealed so it will be watertight)

Design Feature: Round clay pot WITH drain hole, 6-1/2" diam. x 4" deep (does not need to be sealed). Hole can be drilled to accommodate tubing if it does not have a hole.

Filler: Small and medium stones; Bag of natural stone aquarium gravel; **Plants:** Optional moss or fern

Sealants: Sealant for waterproofing (such as epoxy resin); Plumber's Putty, smallest container you can buy

Tools: Serrated kitchen knife

Instructions

1. Measure the diameter of your larger pot approximately 2-1/2" below the rim. Cut a circle from one of the 12" sq. pieces of Plastic foam to this dimension. (Save your scraps; they will be used later.) Cut six equally spaced drainage holes, each slightly larger than a dime, around the perimeter of the foam circle about 3/4" in from the edge. Also cut a notch for the electric cord. Place this circle in the large pot. See Fig. 1. The top of the circle should be about 2-1/2" below the top of the pot. This foam circle does not need to be watertight, just secure enough to hold up the other pot. Some of the discarded foam can be used as wedges under the foam circle to give it more strength and stability.

2. Make sure the drainage hole in the small pot is large enough to accommodate the plastic tubing. Ream out the hole with a drill if it is not.

3. Temporarily position the smaller pot on top of this foam circle. Place it so that it is offset (not centered) and against the position where the electric cord comes out. The top pot should be about 3/4"

Continued on page 102

Instructions (cont.)

from the edge of the large pot. With a pencil, mark the position of the small pot's drainage hole on the plastic foam. Remove the smaller pot and the foam circle.

4. Cut a hole in the plastic foam where you marked. Cut it large enough to accommodate the plastic tubing. This joint does not need to be watertight.

5. Place your pump in the bottom of the larger pot. Position the pump outflow post so that it will approximately line up with the tubing hole you cut in the foam circle. Place the plastic tubing on the pump outlet. Run the tubing through the tubing hole in the foam circle and position the plastic foam in the 10" pot.

6. Measure the inside diameter of the 6-1/2" pot approximately 1" below the rim. Cut a second plastic foam circle to this dimension from the other piece of foam. (Again, save those scraps.) Cut a hole in the center of this circle just barely larger than the diameter of the plastic tubing. This should be a snug fit. If too loose, you can fill in the gap with plumber's putty after final positioning of the circle in the pot. Do a dry fit only now and remove the circle.

7. Run the tubing through the hole in the bottom of the smaller pot. Now place the smaller pot on top of the plastic foam circle in the 10" pot. Slightly tilt the smaller pot away from the near edge (this will be the back edge) of the larger pot by putting a thin scrap of plastic foam under the back edge of the smaller pot. This will cause the water to overflow the smaller pot on the front edge only. Run the tubing through the smaller foam circle. Position the foam circle inside the smaller pot approximately 1" below the rim.

8. The joint between the plastic foam and the clay pot must be watertight, so seal the edge between the two with plumber's putty. Run a moistened finger over the plumber's putty for a smooth joint.

9. Cut the tubing flush with the top of the pot.

10. Stack some of the larger stones toward the back of the top pot behind the tubing. Place other stones around the tubing so that the stones slope slightly from back to front. Fill in any gaps with the aquarium gravel. (Be careful not to get any of the gravel down the plastic tubing.) The stones should be slightly higher than the tubing in the back and flush with it in the front.

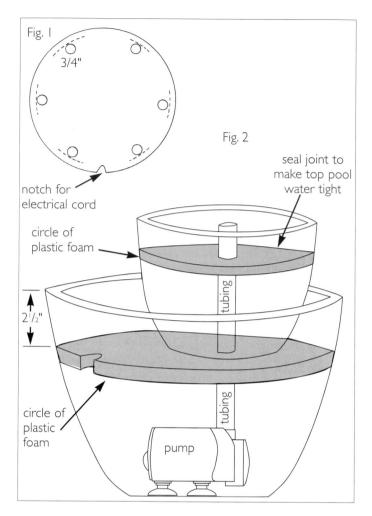

Only the opening of the tubing should be visible.

11. Pour water into the bottom pot through the drainage holes in the foam circle. Be sure the pump is fully submerged.

12. Fill the area between the two pots with the scraps of plastic foam about halfway up to the rim. This is to make the fountain a bit lighter. Do not block the drainage holes in the circle.

13. Cover the plastic foam pieces with stones. After positioning the larger stones, fill in any small gaps with smaller stones and aquarium gravel. If desired, add some sheet moss for decoration.

14. If the water is coming out of the tubing too quickly, adjust the flow control on the pump. (Some disassembly and reassembly will be required.) You may also experiment with the placement of the rocks to get the best sound. ❏

Antique Vase Fountain

Designed by Rhonda Garson

Pictured on pages 104-105

Supplies

Pump: Small fountain submersible pump with outlet on top; 60 GPH @ 1 foot is more than enough performance

Tubing: Flexible plastic tubing to fit the smallest outlet on your pump, 3" length (or more, depending upon the length of your vase)

Container: Plastic terra cotta colored plant saucer, 14" (larger if desired) and deep enough to cover pump

Design Feature: Antique-look vase, size in proportion to saucer (can be any materials in which you can drill a hole; plastic works well and clay would work; does not need to be waterproof)

Filler:

Several sizes of rocks (2 or 3 should be much larger than others; size rocks to fit your saucer);

Sm. bag natural stone aquarium gravel;

Optional florist's glass stones in 2 colors (as many as desired);

Plants: moss (optional)

Sealant: Plumber's Putty

Tools: Drill

Instructions

1. A hole will need to be drilled in the vase to accommodate the outflow post of the pump. The best place to drill this hole is in the widest part of the vase, but not too near the top opening of the vase. Do not drill a hole yet, but keep this in mind as you determine the position of your vase in the saucer. I placed mine off to one side. Remove the vase from saucer.

2. Place the pump in saucer so that it will be directly under the hole drilled in the vase. Run electric cord so it will be in the least visible position.

3. Position the two or three large rocks around the pump to hold it in place and to support the vase. Position the vase on these rocks tilting slightly forward so the water will run out of its mouth (position rocks to get this angle for the vase).

4. Note where the outflow post of the pump contacts the vase. Drill a hole in the vase at this position to accommodate the size of the post. The hole should be *just* large enough for the post to fit snugly.

5. Place the vase on the rocks with the outflow post inserted into the hole in vase. The fit should be fairly tight. It does not have to be completely watertight but should be a snug enough fit that most of the water will run out of the mouth of the vase and not out the hole. If the fit is not tight enough, fill the area around the outlet with a small amount of plumber's putty to make the fit more watertight.

6. You can now place the 3" length of tubing over the outlet inside the vase. The tubing should not touch the top of the vase, so adjust the length as needed. You may need to play with the way the tubing points after you turn the water on, in order to get the best sound and so the water runs out of the vase nicely.

7. Place one medium rock inside the mouth of the vase to help hold it in place. Position the rest of the rocks around the vase to make it more secure. Position a fairly flat rock under the mouth of the vase and place the other rocks in a pleasing arrangement in the saucer. Position the optional florist's glass stones and moss as desired.

8. Fill the saucer with water. Be sure the pump is fully submerged. If your pump has a flow adjustment you may want to start off with it in the medium setting. If that is too low or too high, remove rocks as needed to get to the flow control, make your adjustment, then replace the rocks. ❑

Antique Vase Fountain

Designed by Rhonda Garson

This antique-looking urn is reminiscent of Italian water vessels of long ago. The terra cotta saucer and stones keep with this same country Italian theme. The urn makes this fountain a little more elegant so that it could be placed in most any room — even a traditional living room. A hole is drilled into the side of the urn so that the pump outflow valve can push water into the vase and it can flow out of the mouth and splash onto the rocks.

Insturctions on page 103

Potted Fountain

Designed by Rhonda Garson

There are many ways that clay pots can be used to construct a fountain. Here three clay pots are used in an upright position so that water fills the top pot then cascade down to the next pot. As it fills and overflows, the bottom pot catches the water. The bottom pot is the base container that holds the pump and water. The saucer is used to assure that any splashes do not get onto furniture surfaces. Here the pots were sponged to give them a mossy look.

Supplies

Pump: Small fountain submersible pump with outlet on top; 60 GPH @ 1 foot is more than enough performance

Tubing: Flexible plastic tubing to fit the outflow post on your pump, 12" length; Copper pipe, 1/2" inside diameter (if possible), 3-1/2" length (tubing must fit inside pipe)

Pump Housing: Two pieces of plastic foam (NOT florist's foam!), any color, 1/2" to 1" thick, one piece cut to a 6" circle and one cut to a 4" circle. This will be used to create a space for the pump.

Container: Clay plant pot with no drain hole, 6-3/4" diam. x 5" deep (inside must be sealed so it will be watertight). If you can't find a pot without a drain hole, then the hole can be sealed with silicone caulking.; Large clay saucer

Design Feature: Two clay plant pots WITH a drain hole, 4-1/2" diam. x 4-1/2" deep and 3-1/2" diam. x 2-1/2" deep (these do not need to be sealed)

Filler: Small and medium stones; Bag of natural stone aquarium gravel;

Plants: Moss, fern, or other small plants

Sealants: Sealant for waterproofing (such as epoxy resin); Plumber's Putty, smallest container you can buy

Tools: Serrated kitchen knife; Metal file

Instructions

1. Place pump in center of the 6-3/4" pot. Run the electric cord up and over the back of the pot. If your pump has a flow control setting, start out in the medium position.

2. Cut a hole in the center of the 6" plastic foam circle slightly larger that the diameter of the plastic tubing. This does not need to be a watertight joint. Cut five more equally spaced drainage holes each approximately the size of a dime around the perimeter of the plastic foam circle approximately 3/4" in from edge. Also cut a notch for the electric cord. This foam circle does not need to be watertight, just secure enough to hold up the other pots. The top of the circle should be about 1/2" below the top of the pot.

3. Place the plastic tubing over the outflow post in the top of the pump. Run the tubing through the hole in the center of the 6" foam circle and position the foam in the pot. The electric cord should be in the notch cut for it. The foam should be flat and fit snugly. It should not rest on the pump but be wedged into the pot above the pump. (Some of the discarded pieces of foam can be used as support under the circle if needed.)

4. Make sure the drainage hole in the 4-1/2" pot is large enough for the plastic tubing to fit through. If not, use a knife or a file to enlarge the hole. Place the tubing through the drainage hole in the 4-1/2" pot and sit the pot centered on the foam circle in the bottom pot.

5. Cut a hole in the center of the 4" diameter circle just large enough for the tubing to fit through. This should be a nice snug fit. If the fit is too loose use a small amount of plumber's putty to fill in the gap. Run the tubing through the hole and push the foam circle down into the pot. The top of the circle should be about 1/4" below the top of the pot. The joint between the foam and the clay pot needs to be watertight so seal the edge between the two with plumber's putty. Run a moistened finger over the plumber's putty to get a smooth joint.

6. Next insert the tubing through the drainage hole of the 2-1/2" pot; enlarge as needed. The 2-1/2" pot should then sit on top of the foam circle. Cut the tubing so that it is just below the top of this pot. Insert the copper pipe over the tubing inside the pot. Fill in around the pipe with the aquarium gravel to hold the pipe in place in center of the pot. Fill to just barely below the top of the pot. Place a few small rocks around the copper pipe on top of the aquarium gravel

7. Pour water into the bottom pot through the drainage holes in the foam circle. Be sure the pump is fully submerged. Cover the foam circle with rocks and gravel. First place some of the larger rocks over the drainage holes in the large foam circle, then fill in the empty spaces with smaller rocks and aquarium gravel. Cover the second foam circle with aquarium gravel and a few small rocks. Sit the fountain in the center of the large saucer and fill in around the largest pot with aquarium gravel and rocks.

8. If the water emerges from the copper pipe too quickly, you can gently raise the copper pipe until a better flow is achieved. You can also adjust the flow control on the pump, if needed, but some disassembly and reassembly will be required. You may also experiment with the placement of the rocks to get the best sound. ❑

Candle In the Water

Designed by Kathi Bailey

Pictured on pages 110-111

Supplies

Pump: Mini statuary fountain pump, 90 GPH

Tubing: Clear vinyl tubing, 1/4" diam., 18" length

Container: Square glass bowl, 8" square x at least 6" deep

Design Feature: Square outdoor citronella candle shaped like a granite rock, 6" square

Filler: Two or three flat flagstones; Assorted smooth river rocks, 1/2 lb.

Tools: Metal barbecue skewer, 18" long

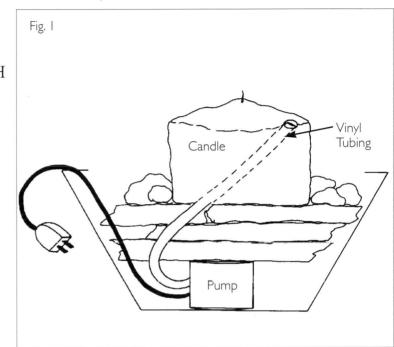

Fig. I

Candle

Vinyl Tubing

Pump

Instructions

1. Mark candle at top front edge and again at bottom back (see Fig. 1). Heat end of skewer over stove or flame for 30 seconds. Insert skewer into top front mark on candle at an angle toward back mark and push. Repeat with reheating and inserting skewer into candle until it comes out through bottom back mark. Rotate skewer to insure that hole is at least 1/4" in diameter.

2. Insert vinyl tubing through top of candle and out through bottom. Pull until top end of tubing is where you want it. If you want water to flow gently from the opening, place the top end of tubing approximately 1/4" down in hole from top of candle. If you want a stronger flow, position top end of tubing flush with top of candle.

3. Attach other (bottom) end of tubing onto pump and place pump at bottom of bowl.

4. Add flat stones on top of the pump. Stack enough flat stones so that you have only about 1" above stones to top of bowl.

5. Place top of candle on stones and add additional rocks to hide tubing. See Fig. 1

6. Add water to bowl, plug in pump, and adjust the water flow.

NOTES: Candle may be lit if water flow is gentle and will not interfere with flame. When candle burns down and forms a well, place a votive candle there. Votive candle can be replaced as it burns down, allowing the "granite rock" candle to remain intact. ❑

Candle in the Water

Designed by Kathi Bailey

A candle that looks like a piece of granite is used as the design feature of this fountain. A hole is drilled in the candle so that the plastic tubing can bring the water up to the top of the candle. Water flows out of the top of the candle and cascades down the candle into the bottom container. To keep the candle from burning down and getting shorter, a small tea light or votive candle can be placed in the center of the candle and lit instead of the normal candle wick.

Fount From the Faucet

Designed by Kathi Bailey

This fountain will add a bit of whimsy to your surroundings. Place this fountain against a wall of your porch or patio and your guests will think you have forgotten to turn off your water. Then they will wonder why the bucket never overflows. The soothing water sounds make it appealing for back porch relaxing.

Supplies

Pump: Mini statuary fountain pump, 90 GPH

Tubing: Clear vinyl tubing, 1/4" diam., 2 ft. length

Container/Design Feature: Metal wall hanging bucket, 6" wide x 18" high

Design Feature: Hose bibb, 1/2" (faucet)

Hardware: Electrical conduit fitting, 1/2"

Filler: Two or three flat flagstones; Assorted smooth river rocks, 1/2 lb.

Sealant: Silicone adhesive or flexible industrial strength adhesive

Tools: Electric drill with 1/2" bit; Tin snips; Screwdriver

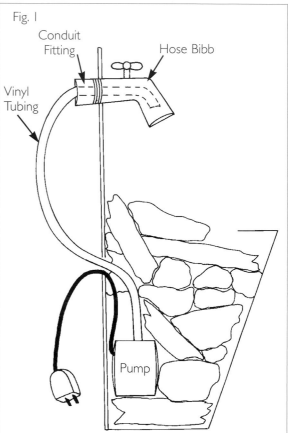

Instructions

1. Test bucket for waterproofing. If any water leaks, seal it with glue and let set overnight.

2. Insert vinyl tubing into hose bibb so that water will pour from the faucet at front. It may be necessary to remove handle to insert tubing all the way through the bibb. See Fig. 1.

3. Drill a hole approximately 1-1/2" down from top on back piece of bucket. Insert back of hose bibb from front and attach to back with conduit fitting. (Use tin snips to enlarge hole, if necessary). Make sure that excess tubing comes down back of bucket.

4. Drill second hole approximately 6" up from bottom at back. Make sure this hole will be ABOVE your water line but below the top of your bucket portion. Enlarge hole with tin snips to fit plug from pump into it. Insert end of clear tubing from back into bucket (Fig. 1). Place pump in bucket and insert plug through hole out to back. Attach tubing to pump.

5. Add flagstones and assorted river rocks on top of pump and up to top of bucket line.

6. Fill with water to BELOW drilled hole. Plug in pump and adjust water flow from faucet onto rocks. ❑

The Old Urn

This fountain is larger than tabletop. It makes a wonderful fountain to use on a protected porch or patio. Water gurgles up and fills the urn, then cascades over the sides to the bottom washtub.

Supplies

Pump: Submersible pump
Tubing: Plastic tubing, 3/8" x 12" long
Pump housing: Two bricks
Container: Galvanized washtub, approximately 18" diameter
Design Feature: Large metal urn with metal base
Filler: Slate rocks
Sealant: silicone adhesive
Tools: Drill

Instructions

1. Drill a hole into the bottom of the urn and base to accommodate plastic tubing. This urn is metal so it is easy to drill. Thread a piece of plastic tubing into urn and seal around tubing with silicone caulking.

2. Place two bricks in the bottom of the washtub with a space between them to accommodate the pump. Place the pump between the bricks.

3. Place the urn on top of the two bricks. Place the end of the tubing coming out the bottom of the urn onto the outflow post on the pump. Trim top of plastic tubing if needed.

4. Place slate stones in washtub to hide the pump and the bricks.

5. Fill washtub with water. Turn on pump and let the pump fill up the urn. Add more water to keep the pump submerged. When water fills the urn and begins to overflow into washtub, then you can stop adding water. ❏

Exotic Bamboo

Designed by Kathi Bailey

Reminiscent of a Japanese water garden, this fountain is especially exotic. Be sure to find a container that keeps with the Oriental theme of this fountain. You will need to adjust water flow so that it stays within the bowl.

Supplies

Pump: Mini statuary fountain pump, 90 GPH

Tubing: Clear vinyl tubing, 1/4" diam., 2 ft. length

Pump Housing: Block floral foam, 10" square (to create space for pump); Two or three flat flagstones

Container: Ceramic bowl, 9" diam. x at least 9" deep

Design Feature: Bamboo, 1-1/2" diam., 18" length

Filler: Assorted smooth river rocks, 1/2 lb.; Spanish moss

Sealant: Silicone adhesive or Flexible industrial strength adhesive

Tools: Hand saw; Rotary drill; Screwdriver; Sharp knife

Instructions

1. Cut bamboo into one 4" length and one 10" length. Study the bamboo so that you can cut each piece where it will be hollow and with no walls or nodes occurring within the piece. Cut one end of each piece at a 30-degree angle.

2. The 10" piece will be your standing tower. Measure down 2" from top (end that is cut on an angle) and cut a hole 1" to 1-1/2" in diameter (depending on diameter of your bamboo) in one side of the bamboo. Insert the flat end of the 4" bamboo piece into this hole and glue to secure.

3. Cut floral foam to fit into bowl, allowing space at side of bowl for pump. Use a screw-driver to insert a hole for tubing in floral foam from top back to lower back (see Fig. 1). Insert vinyl tubing through floral foam. Insert bottom of bamboo tower into foam (Fig. 1). Continue running top of tubing up through bamboo tower and through the short piece of bamboo (spout).

4. Insert foam base into bowl. Place pump in bowl. Attach tubing to pump. Add flat stones to cover pump and foam.

5. Place river rocks on top of foam around bamboo. Glue Spanish moss around bamboo.

6. Add water, being sure to compensate for the amount soaked up by floral foam. Plug in pump and adjust water flow from bamboo spout. ❏

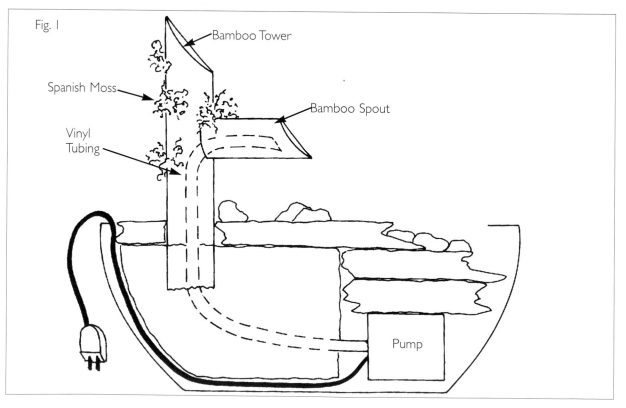

Fig. 1
Bamboo Tower
Spanish Moss
Bamboo Spout
Vinyl Tubing
Pump

Cup & Saucers Fountain

Designed by Kathi Bailey

Pictured on page 120 & 121

Supplies

Pump: Mini statuary fountain pump, 90 GPH

Tubing: Clear vinyl tubing, 1/4" diam., 10" length

Pump Housing: Two or three flat flagstones

Container: Ceramic or acrylic bowl, 12" diam. x at least 4" deep

Design Feature: China cup; Three china saucers, coordinating colors (available inexpensively at flea markets or thrift stores); 6" floral foam block

Filler: Assorted smooth river rocks, 1/2 lb.

Sealant: Silicone adhesive or Flexible industrial strength adhesive

Tools: Needlenose pliers

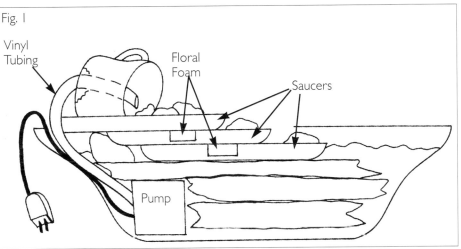

Instructions

1. If saucers aren't the same size, place them with the largest at bottom and smallest at top. Cut a 1" x 1" x 1/2" piece of floral foam and glue in center bottom on topside of largest saucer. Glue second saucer on top, angled down toward the front and overlapping back half of bottom saucer. Glue a 1" x 1" x 1/2" piece of floral foam in center on topside of middle saucer. Glue third saucer on top, angled down toward the front and overlapping back half of middle saucer. Saucers must be angled so that water will run down them.

2. Use needlenose pliers to break a 1" piece off side of cup so it will sit level in saucer (refer to Fig. 1). Drill a 1/2" hole at base of cup. Glue cup to top saucer so that hole is at back and broken niche is at bottom front.

3. Insert tubing through hole in cup, allowing 1-1/2" to protrude inside cup toward front.

4. Place pump in bowl. Attach bottom of vinyl tubing to pump. Lay two or three flat stones beside and on top of pump to raise bottom saucer up to top of bowl. See Fig. 1.

5. Add assorted rocks around saucers on top of flagstones. Glue additional rocks to saucers and cup and around the vinyl tubing inside cup to hide it.

6. Add water to submerge pump. Plug in pump and adjust water flow and tubing as needed. ❑

Cup & Saucers Fountain

Designed by Kathi Bailey

Friends will giggle when they admire your fountain because it may remind them of the sink-full of dirty dishes they left behind. Choose some interesting china to add to the appeal of this fountain.

Duck Pond

Designed by Kathi Bailey

This is a handsome fountain for a man's desk. A piece of fish statuary would be a good substitute for the duck. If you can't drill a hole in the statuary, you could have the tube come up out of the rocks just beside the statuary to create a spout.

Supplies

Pump: Mini statuary fountain pump, 90 GPH

Tubing: Clear vinyl tubing, 1/4" diam., 8" length

Pump Housing: Two or three flat flagstones placed above pump

Container: Ceramic bowl, 8" diam. x at least 4" deep

Design Feature: Small hollow resin duck statue

Filler: Assorted smooth river rocks, 1/2 lb.

Plants: Pkg. dried cat o' nine tails; 2" square of floral foam

Tools: Electric drill with 1/4" bit; Sharp knife or flat head screwdriver

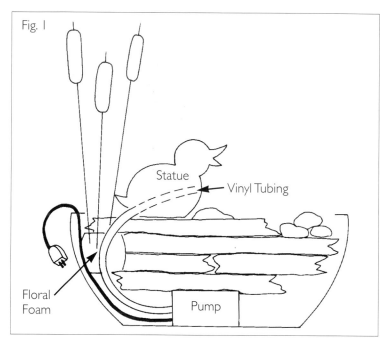

Instructions

1. Drill a hole through duck for tubing.

2. Insert tubing into hole so that end is flush with duck's mouth (or front of statue if using some other type statue). Attach other end of tubing to pump.

3. Refer to Fig. 1. Place pump in bottom of bowl. Add flat stones to cover pump. Place statue on top of stones at back.

4. Add a small piece of floral foam at back of dish to cover tubing. Insert cat o' nine tails into floral foam.

5. Add river rocks on top of flat rocks. Add more cat o' nine tails as desired.

6. Fill bowl with water, being sure to compensate for the amount soaked up by floral foam. Plug in pump and adjust water flow. ❏

Gooseneck Lamp Fountain

Designed by Kathi Bailey

A hollow gooseneck plastic lamp was the perfect receptacle for the plastic tubing. The water spills out the top and splashes onto the rocks below. A climbing plant helps disguise the lamp.

Supplies

Pump: Mini statuary fountain pump, 90 GPH

Tubing: Clear vinyl tubing, 1/4" diam., 2 ft. length

Pump Housing: Two or three flat flagstones placed above pump

Container: Ceramic bowl, 9" diam. x at least 4" deep

Design Feature: Gooseneck lamp, 18" tall with maximum 6" diam. base

Filler: Assorted smooth river rocks, 1/2 lb.;

Plant: Philodendron plant

Tools: Wire cutter; Philips head screwdriver

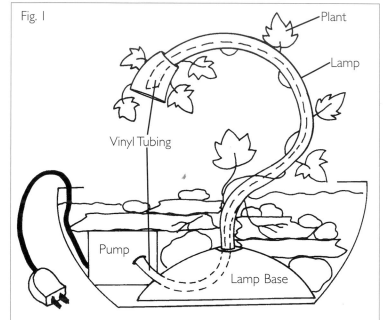

Instructions

1. Remove lamp shade, electrical wiring, and cord from lamp. Insert vinyl tubing up through gooseneck (replacing cord) to where the bulb would be.
2. Set pump inside bowl. Attach bottom end of tubing to pump. Place base of gooseneck inside bowl beside pump. Place flat rocks on top of pump and base of lamp. Add additional flagstones and assorted river rocks on top.
3. Curve lamp neck so that water will fall down onto rocks.
4. Place plant among rocks.
5. Fill bowl with water. Plug in the pump. Make sure roots of plant are in water. Trim plant as it grows. ❏

METRIC CONVERSION CHART

Inches to Millimeters and Centimeters

Inches	MM	CM
1/8	3	.3
1/4	6	.6
3/8	10	1.0
1/2	13	1.3
5/8	16	1.6
3/4	19	1.9
7/8	22	2.2
1	25	2.5
1-1/4	32	3.2
1-1/2	38	3.8
1-3/4	44	4.4
2	51	5.1
3	76	7.6
4	102	10.2
5	127	12.7
6	152	15.2
7	178	17.8
8	203	20.3
9	229	22.9
10	254	25.4
11	279	27.9
12	305	30.5

Yards to Meters

Yards	Meters
1/8	.11
1/4	.23
3/8	.34
1/2	.46
5/8	.57
3/4	.69
7/8	.80
1	.91
2	1.83
3	2.74
4	3.66
5	4.57
6	5.49
7	6.40
8	7.32
9	8.23
10	9.14

INDEX

INDEX